Reprints of Economic Classics

NARRATIVE

OF

THE CONDITION

OF THE

MANUFACTURING POPULATION

NARRATIVE

OF

THE CONDITION

OF THE

MANUFACTURING POPULATION

AND THE

PROCEEDINGS OF GOVERNMENT

WHICH LEAD TO THE

State Trials in Scotland

BY

ALEXANDER B. RICHMOND

[1824]

REPRINTS OF ECONOMIC CLASSICS

AUGUSTUS M. KELLEY · PUBLISHERS

NEW YORK 1971

First Edition 1824

(London: *Printed for* John Miller, *New Bridge Street, Blackfriars*, 1824)

Reprinted 1971 by

AUGUSTUS M. KELLEY · PUBLISHERS

REPRINTS OF ECONOMIC CLASSICS

New York New York 10001

. . . .

I S B N 0 678 00676 8

L C N 68 56571

. . . .

PRINTED IN THE UNITED STATES OF AMERICA

by SENTRY PRESS, NEW YORK, N. Y. 10019

NARRATIVE

OF

THE CONDITION

OF THE

MANUFACTURING POPULATION;

AND

THE PROCEEDINGS OF GOVERNMENT

WHICH LED TO THE

State Trials in Scotland,

FOR ADMINISTERING UNLAWFUL OATHS, AND THE SUSPENSION OF THE HABEAS CORPUS ACT, IN 1817, WITH A DETAILED ACCOUNT OF THE SYSTEM OF ESPIONAGE ADOPTED AT THAT PERIOD,

IN GLASGOW AND ITS NEIGHBOURHOOD.

ALSO,

A SUMMARY

OF SIMILAR PROCEEDINGS, IN OTHER PARTS OF THE COUNTRY,

TO THE

EXECUTION OF THISTLEWOOD AND OTHERS,

FOR HIGH TREASON, IN 1820.

BY ALEX. B. RICHMOND.

"Who steals my purse, steals trash. 'Tis something—nothing.
'Twas mine—'tis his—and has been slave to thousands;
But he that filches from me my good name,
Robs me of that which not enriches him,
And makes me poor indeed." SHAKSPEARE.

"The worst thing I could wish to my worst enemy is, that his character should become the *subject* of vindication."—GODWIN.

LONDON:

PRINTED FOR JOHN MILLER,

NEW BRIDGE-STREET, BLACKFRIARS.

1824.

PREFACE.

I SHALL offer no apology for submitting the following Narrative of Facts to public inspection, being convinced I am performing an important and imperative duty to society, as well as to myself. In deference to the opinion of others, and contrary to my own, I have delayed publication, I believe, greatly to the prejudice of my own interest and character, and it now remains to be seen who was in the right, or who had most cause to be afraid of publicity. If the excitement has gone past, the time is favourable for forming a more impartial judgment, it being neither too proximate nor too remote from the occurrences; and I trust it will be found I have neither extenuated, nor set down ought in malice, to gratify either individual or party. Setting up no literary pretensions, I only pledge myself to having steadily adhered to the truth, in a plain unvarnished Statement of Facts, as far as they occurred within my own knowledge. In doing so, I have not violated even an implied promise with a single person; and, as an evidence that I have taken no undue advantage, the proof sheets were offered to all the parties, materially interested, before they were put to press. I consider I have brought forward all the persons in a sufficiently prominent manner, to enable the Public to come to a just decision; and if an attempt is made to invalidate any of my statements, written documents, and still more special references, are forthcoming, to confirm them, if called for.

The march of improvement has hitherto been materially impeded by government's endeavouring to throw an impenetrable veil of mystery over their proceedings; although society has no security against the recurrence of evil equal to a full development of past errors. From the days of Beccario I should think it difficult to find an enlightened individual, who would not prefer the prevention to the punishment of crime; but it is a very nice point to distinguish and decide upon, how far the means of prevention should be allowed to violate the sanctuary of private life, or trench upon individual liberty. Upon that point men's minds have been, and will be, various; and as much has been said, written, and conjectured, on the present subject, I am well aware conclusions will be drawn, according as opinion coincides with, or dissents from, the different views taken of that question. As I have no room for remarks upon the general principle, from those who have formerly known me I solicit a candid retrospect of their former sentiments. Personal vindication is always a painful and frequently an invidious task, and it ought to be remembered, there is little merit in a sacrifice that is certain of commanding the general sympathy of society, compared to one made at the hazard of encountering its strongest and deepest rooted prejudices. I may have been guilty of errors in judgment, but to no man, nor set of men, will I concede a more ardent desire to do good, either in the acts and deeds I have performed, or in now submitting the detail of them to the world; and, in the language of the late Mr. Curran, if I have contributed to preserve the memory of other acts and actors, that ought not to be buried in oblivion, my labour will not have been without its use.

NARRATIVE,

&c. &c.

Since the publication of Smith's Wealth of Nations, many eminent writers have been engaged in illustrating the principles of political economy and pointing out the leading circumstances which promote or retard the accumulation of national wealth. The discoveries and improvements made during the same period in the exact sciences, tending to supersede and abridge human labour, have called forth energies and produced results which have astonished the present age, and set at nought the calculations of the most acute and profound philosophers and politicians of former times. In our own country almost a total revolution has been effected in the whole frame of society; capital and the means of producing all the luxuries of life have been augmented, perhaps, in a tenfold ratio; yet it is questionable if, in the midst of all this apparent improvement, the substantial comfort and happiness of the great body of the people have in any degree been promoted, and whether the enlightened philanthropist will not consider they have rather retrograded.

The theorists in political economy attach more importance to the aggregate accumulation of wealth and power than to the manner of its diffusion, or its effects on the interior of society. The manufacturer possessed of capital, and the inventor of a new machine, study only how to turn them to their own profit and advantage; the statesman considers every improvement important only as it augments the national resources, relative to other countries; but, in all these calculations, the effect produced on the condition of the labourer has been no more valued than a transfer of negroes on the estate of a West India planter, or boors on that of a Russian nobleman. Proceeding on this principle, England, for several years presented, the anomalous spectacle, of a country saturated with wealth and abounding in every superfluity, with the mass of her efficient labouring population, in the midst of profound peace, unable, even by excessive exertion, to command the bare necessaries of life.

It is not my intention to enter generally into the causes which have produced this state of things, or to show their effects on the country at large; but the positive sufferings and discontents of the labouring classes, resulting from that system, having rendered it imperative on me to publish the present narrative, it is necessary to take a retrospective view of its progress in our cotton manufactures, for the purpose of showing the actual condition of the manufacturing districts in Scotland, in 1816 and 1817; the means I had of acquiring a knowledge of that condition, and to account for the connexions I had formed in society, which involved me, as a party, in the public measures of that period.

For the last forty years, the ablest writers on political science have been advocates for a general freedom of trade, and have condemned the whole system of bounties, prohibitory duties, monopolies and restrictions of all kinds; leaving every thing open to fair competition. The greater part of their reasoning, however, more immediately refers to the external trade of one country compared with that of another; and few of them have been aware of the effect produced by the application of the principle on the different classes of the same community, or the positive injustice done, by its operating in one case and not in another. It is indeed a delicate point to interfere with, being the keystone of the whole political machine; for, were the principle generally applied, it would change the whole order of society and annihilate all the incorporated and chartered rights of the country. Thus we have a number of small communities, enjoying particular privileges, forming the component parts of a larger; and the *benefits* of this boasted freedom of trade are confined to those who have no special privileges to defend, or have not the means of doing so.

It is both a curious and important subject of investigation, how far the different branches of manufacture have been influenced by the facilities and obstructions which have arisen out of this state of society. I have met with no writer who has given any good reason why the manufacture of the exotic cotton has been carried to such an unparalleled extent, in preference to articles of native growth, or why we have not, long ago, been able to supply half the globe with hats, &c. as well as muslins. The inventions of Watt, Arkwright and Crompton will not altogether account for this; for those and other discoveries would have perhaps given equal facility to many other branches. I shall therefore state what appears to me to have had a very powerful influence in giving this ascendency, which will also account for the unprecedented fluctuations and ultimate permanent depression of the price of labour in the cotton manufacture.

The reign of Elizabeth may be said to have given birth to manufactures in England; also to monopolies, special privileges and immunities, many of which still continue to exercise a strong influence on different branches of trade and manufacture, and perhaps none more so than the acts passed to enforce apprenticeships. Since the repeal or dissuetude of these acts, the principle which they established and the impulse which they gave has been kept up by conventional agreements, in various trades and professions, to seclude all who have not served a certain period, or paid certain premiums; and these restrictions have the same effect in preventing a trade from being overstocked with hands as positive law. It is also an indisputable fact, where these regulations have been strictly adopted, the price of labour has been kept higher and subject to less fluctuation; nor does it appear to have diminished the relative profit of the master; although it has uniformly operated against the extension of the trade*. No fault can justly be found, however, with the mechanic, or artisan, for adhering to such restrictions as are calculated to promote the interest of his own particular branch. The time and money he has spent in acquiring his skill are his capital, which he is equally entitled to preserve and improve as the members of the church or the law; and it is an invasion of natural right to prevent him from doing so, until all laws, conferring special privileges, are abrogated.

The cotton manufacture was attempted, in Scotland, previous to the Union, but was chiefly confined to mixed goods, England herself not being able, for long after, to meet the Indian com-

* An accurate history of the various trades and professions would be a valuable acquisition, and is yet a desideratum in political economy. We have abundance of theories and now want an accumulation of facts; but it would require a person intimately acquainted with the labouring classes and, at the same time, above their prejudices, which has not yet been the case with any writer on the science.

petition in muslins. Little progress was, however, made until about the end of the American revolutionary war, from which period a number of concurring circumstances have contributed to its increase and extension, with a degree of rapidity altogether unexampled in the history of society. In 1787, the total estimated annual value of this branch of manufacture was 890,000*l*.*; it is now near 40 millions, a sum greater than the whole trade and manufacture of the country at the first period, and it is still rapidly increasing.

To enumerate all the circumstances that have contributed to open a market for this widely-extended branch of manufacture, would be to give a history of the last forty years, which is foreign to my purpose, my chief aim being, to point out such only as appear to me to have given facility to its extension and the progressive change in the condition of the people employed. Arkwright's discovery was unquestionably the first great stimulus given, and the commencement of the cotton manufacture may be said to have been coeval with that invention, any thing previously done being comparatively trifling. In Scotland, nature pointed out Glasgow and Paisley as the most eligible places for its establishment. The local advantages consisted in the cheapness of coal and iron; a numerous resident population, with the price of labour comparatively low, and where emigrants could, with facility, be drawn from the adjoining counties, the West Highlands and Ireland. The situation was also favourable for carrying on an extensive foreign trade with America and the West Indies. Similar local advantages established it in Lancashire. This occurred at a time when the spirit of improvement had been consi-

* Vide the Scots Magazine for 1787.

derably diffused among the agricultural classes, and the adoption of the system of large farms left the small farmer and cottager no alternative but to take refuge in the towns, or in emigration*; by which means the increasing demand for labourers was easily supplied. But that which, above all other causes, contributed to the extension of this branch of manufacture, (though little noticed,) was the almost unrestricted freedom of admission. Paisley had, as early as from 1760 to 1770, carried the manufacture of silk gauze and some other fabrics, to such a degree of perfection as to rival Spitalfields, and even the French, in their own markets; but, although there were upwards of five thousand looms employed, they never established any regular system of apprenticeships, terms being altogether arbitrary. When that branch was superseded by the cotton, the same principle prevailed; and, when the demand for labourers increased, even adults were taught, for a few pounds, without any apprenticeship, and whole families were employed in the spinning department, without giving any gratuity whatever for teaching. The money-price of manufacturing was considerably above that paid to agricultural labourers; and another great inducement to engage in the weaving department arose from the workmen being employed in their own houses, altogether independent of the masters, as to hours of labour; it also afforded many facilities to the workmen to become masters, with little or no capital.

It might have been obvious, that this universal freedom of admission, compared with other pro-

* This deprived the country of a race of men whose loss must be deplored by every lover of simplicity of manners, and whose moral worth will never be compensated by all the splendour and riches of our manufacturing system.

fessions, would have a tendency to reduce the price of labour, by producing a redundancy of hands; but, before it attracted the attention of the operatives, whose interests were more deeply concerned, the body was too unwieldy to be managed by conventional regulation. Indeed, the first attempt made, was one of direct resistance to the reduction of prices, and not the adoption of measures calculated to keep them up by the more indirect, but safer method, of regulating the proportion of hands to the demand. This occurred, in Scotland, as early as 1787, and was the first rupture between the masters and workmen. The fabrics, at that time introduced, were few in number and were respectively paid, by the masters, at one uniform price; but from the difficulty of forming a proper estimate of a new branch of manufacture, they were all rated too high, and, in that year, the masters combined to reduce them. The new scale, proposed by them, was considered too low, by the workmen, and a negotiation took place, to adjust the difference, which ultimately failed, and a counter combination was the consequence. Meetings of the whole body of operatives were held in Glasgow, and resolutions adopted to expel those masters from the trade who had become most obnoxious, for having taken a lead in the reduction, by not working for them at any price; also, to force their own body to comply with these measures, and not to work for other masters *under* a price fixed by themselves. The contest continued for some time, until a part of the workmen, (unwilling or unable to remain unemployed,) taking work at the masters' prices, were compelled, by their brethren, to return it; and, in many instances, it was burnt and destroyed. They continued to assemble, in large bodies, parading the streets, and, on the magistrates attempting to apprehend the ringleaders, they were resisted, the riot act was read, the military called in to the assistance of the civil power, and, the workmen not dispersing, several were killed and others mortally wounded. Prosecutions followed, which ultimately broke up the combination, and the operatives were obliged to submit to any terms the masters chose to impose.

This era is chiefly remarkable for having put an end to uniformity of price for the same fabrics, and opened a field for individual speculation on the price of labour, without example, in this or any other country. A table of prices was drawn up and published, in 1792, by some of the leading houses in the trade, embracing all the fabrics then introduced, but it never was uniformly acted on; deviations from it were progressively made, and it soon became only a nominal standard of reference. The commencement of the French revolutionary war, the following year, produced the first great reaction and depression, and, for the first time, exhibited, on a large scale, the vicissitudes which a manufacturing population, whose products depended upon foreign consumption, were exposed to.

Up to about the year 1800, things went on in a similar manner; the trade was rapidly increasing, and every fluctuation and depression only seemed to give it renovated elasticity. Many new fabrics were introduced, together with new combinations of the old; but it was still conducted on the same principle. The money-price had been progressively on the decline, but many improvements to expedite labour had been made, and a new race had sprung up, inured to sedentary employments and more constant and severe application than their fathers. The high price of provisions, from 1799 to 1801, had the same effect, in depriving the workmen of comforts, as a reduction in the price of labour, trade, at the same time, being considerably depressed. The system of unequal payments had also become quite general, and various other abuses had crept in, by litigating cases at law, when differences occurred, or disputes arose, between the masters and workmen. The attention of the more reflecting part of the trade was aroused: general measures were adopted, to correct the growing evils, and both kingdoms ultimately joined, in an application to parliament for relief. Petitions were presented for a bill to regulate apprenticeships, to fix a minimum on the price of labour and to settle all disputes, arising between masters and workmen, by arbitration. The two first points were, however, abandoned, and parliament, after an investigation by a committee, granted the third, by passing two bills, one for England and another for Scotland, known by the name of the Arbitration Acts. The principle of those bills is nearly the same; they regulate the description and manner of giving out work, and settle all disputes, arising between parties, by summary process, before the justices, who are empowered to appoint arbitrators, from whose decision there is no appeal*. Every thing else, however, remained as before, and, notwithstanding the regular drain of men, to supply the army and navy, the number of hands were, upon the average of times, pressing against the means of employment. Weaving by machinery had also come into partial operation, which had the same effect as an increase of hands, and a regular and systematic speculation on the price of labour followed, subjecting it, like the public funds, to daily fluctuation.

* These bills, which were passed in 1803, are the only legislative measures ever adopted respecting the cotton trade. A similar bill was extended to Ireland in 1813.

The ease with which credit was obtained, enabled men to get into the trade with little or no capital, who, in general, were foremost in the race of reduction. Many of the older and more respectable houses, tinctured with the prejudices of the olden time, lagged behind and were for taking into consideration the comforts and condition of the workmen, but they were soon compelled to overtake their more enlightened and more energetic competitors, or quit the business. The instability and insecurity, resulting from this state of things, produced universal dissatisfaction among all classes of the workmen. The price of stock in hand being also affected by every fluctuation, many (perhaps a majority) of the masters and wholesale merchants were equally anxious that some regulation should be adopted, which would enable them to carry on their operations with a greater degree of certainty as to ultimate profits, the price of finished goods being comparatively little affected by variations in the price of the raw material. The trade were, however, too much divided in opinion and interest to afford any prospect of an agreement among themselves. It was therefore resolved to apply directly to parliament, and petitions were presented in the session of 1808-9, praying for a bill to affix a minimum on the price of labour. The principle of a minimum was not new, for, independent of the general law, then existing, empowering justices of the peace to affix rates of wages, it was specially recognized, in the case of the silk trade of the metropolis, by a bill, regulating both the price of labour and apprenticeships, which had been in operation from 1773*.

* This bill was repealed last session of parliament, in consequence of the trade of the metropolis not being able to meet the competition in the country, without materially lowering the price of labour. The effect upon the condition of the people remains to be seen, and may be easily foretold.

England and Scotland joined in the application, and deputations were sent from both, composed of persons, from all branches of the trade, to be examined by a committee of the House of Commons, to whom the petitions were referred. Merchants, commission-agents, manufacturers and operatives were examined, and their evidence was decisive as to the existence of the evil and the cause. It was also decidedly favourable to the principle of a minimum, under proper regulations, as the most probable remedy for effecting a cure; but the theoretical opinions, of the advantages to be derived from unrestricted and universal freedom in trade, were spread too widely and were too deeply rooted in the minds of the members of the House, to induce them to try the experiment; for, without particularly attending to the consistency of their legislation, they finally rejected the application. The reason assigned for this was, that it would be ruinous to the operatives, by restricting the trade and thereby throwing them out of employment.

While the deputies remained in London, they had frequent conferences with a number of the members of both Houses of Parliament, many of whom evinced great anxiety to ameliorate the condition of the operatives. Among these the late Mr. Whitbread and Mr. Curwen were conspicuous; and in conversations which those gentlemen held with the operative deputies, after their application had proved abortive, they gave it as their opinion, that, however desirable it might be to have some regulation which would insure the comfort and render the condition of the operatives more stable, there was no hope of obtaining those advantages by legislative enactment; and that the speculative opinions of the age were opposed to any such interference. They therefore advised, that an effort should be made to adopt and enforce some regulation which would prevent the indiscriminate admission of hands into the trade; a remedy which, in time, might regulate the number to suit the demand, and operate as a check upon such ruinous fluctuations. Mr. Whitbread, in particular, enforced the adoption of such a measure and illustrated its propriety by examples from his own experience, where parties, engaged in the same branch of business, fixed the rate of wages, as well as the price of commodities by mutual agreement.

On their return home, the deputies disseminated those opinions, and, although it was an herculean task to reconcile so many contending interests, and to get a body, now become so numerous, to agree upon any given plan, it was determined to make the attempt. Many of the master manufacturers and capitalists, engaged in various branches of the trade, were friendly to the measure, and gave it their support; but success could only be commanded by the united exertion and mutual co-operation of the whole body of operatives. England had priority in the esablishment, and has always had the largest share of this manufacture; but Scotland has long had the most ingenious part of the weaving department, and by far the most valuable, in proportion to the number of looms; and the superior education and intelligence of her workmen, resulting from her parochial institutions, gave them a proportionate ascendency, in all joint measures, for their mutual benefit. In this instance, Scotland took a decided lead, and Glasgow, in place of Manchester, became the centre of active operations; articles were drawn up, not to allow any person to get into the trade without serving a regular apprenticeship, which was afterwards fixed at seven years; also to restrict the number to be taken by one person; regulate the transfer of journeymen and prevent frauds and embezzlement. The whole, together with addresses to the trade, were published in the newspapers and otherwise printed and circulated, and delegates were sent to all the manufacturing towns and villages, to impress upon the minds of the people the necessity and propriety of their adoption.

At this period I began to take an active interest in promoting these objects, and, although the personal pronoun may be offensive to many, as it is disagreeable to my own feelings, it is necessary, for a right understanding of transactions, in which I filled so prominent a part, that it should be used without reserve; and that names, dates and circumstances should also be particularly condescended upon. With a proportion of speculative and experimental knowledge at least equal to my situation and a decided friend to popular rights, I had (by residing some time in Ireland) witnessed the condition and been enabled to form a judgement of the degradation resulting from the mass of a population being pressed down to the lowest species of food; and conceiving that causes were in active operation which would soon place our manufacturing population in a similar condition, I considered it my duty to lend my assistance to preserve them from a fate which appeared to me inevitable. I entered into the measures of the period with avidity and enthusiasm, and with sanguine hopes as to the practicability of the scheme; but, with those who had entertained similar opinions, found, in the sequel, that we had overrated our powers. It was obious that the first thing to be done was, to convince the body of operatives that the preservation of their relative condition depended upon their numbers being kept down to the real demands of the trade. Next, when they adopted regulations, calculated to effect that purpose, that they should see them rigidly enforced; but, as they were scattered over a great many towns and villages, it required a general system of "*surveillance*" to prevent frauds and deceptions, for which purpose affiliated societies were formed, on the following principle: The large towns were divided into districts, consisting of a certain number of looms; each village forming a distinct district; these districts were again subdivided, according to circumstances, and one or more persons appointed to superintend them; the whole of whom formed a local committee, with power to call general meetings, when any exigency required. Central committees (composed of delegates from a number of districts) were formed, in Scotland, at Glasgow, Paisley and Perth; in England, at Manchester, Bolton, Preston, Carlisle, &c. and, in Ireland, at Belfast, between whom a constant and active correspondence was kept up. In Glasgow a weekly meeting was held, composed of delegates from as many of the surrounding districts as could conveniently attend, who had the power of settling all disputes that arose in the districts, of proposing amendments and alterations in the laws, and calling general meetings of delegates from all the districts in Scotland. The expence was borne by an equal assessment, regular books were kept, and the greatest anxiety was shown to conduct every thing legally, the crown lawyers being furnished with printed copies of the articles and regulations. This association, which commenced in the year 1809, required great exertion to mature; and the organization was almost perfect at the close of 1812, when it was finally broken up, by the interference of government. I shall therefore go on to relate its proceedings and the cause and manner of its dissolution.

The operation of the Berlin and Milan Decrees had, for a considerable time, almost annihilated our direct trade with the Continent of Europe, and our Orders in Council (a retaliatory measure) had recoiled upon ourselves, and placed us in nearly a similar situation with the United States of America. Our foreign trade being thus greatly curtailed and forced into indirect and circuitous channels, during the year 1810, produced an unusual number of bankruptcies, which were followed, in 1811, with an unprecedented fall in the price of manufacturing labour. The price of provisions was, at the same time, very high, which greatly aggravated the distress, and, it being found difficult to carry the internal regulations into full effect, and the advantages, to be derived from them, too remote to meet the present exigency, it was resolved to make another appeal to parliament for relief. This application was made by Scotland alone, in name of the manufacturing and trading interest, as opposed to the agricultural. Communications were opened with all the other trades and professions, to ascertain their condition, and the petition was presented in name of the whole. The ground of argument was, the laws restricting the trade in corn, which, it was contended, had the same effect in supporting its price (when there was a deficiency of home produce) as affixing a minimum on manufacturing labour, and equally a violation of the principle of non-interference. The petitioners prayed for relief generally, and suggested a bill, similar to that regulating the silk trade of the metropolis. Deputies were sent up and examined, at considerable length, by a committee of the House of Commons; but, for the same reason assigned in 1809, parliament declared they would not interfere.

All hope of parliamentary interference was now given up, and a general gloom pervaded the whole operative part of the trade; their condition appeared almost hopeless, nor have they ever regained the relative situation they held previous to 1810. Improvements, in weaving by machinery, were advancing with giant strides, and the poverty of the operatives has tended to perpetuate and enhance the evil of their condition, by depriving them of the means of putting their families into any other profession. A gleam of hope sprung up and illumined the horizon during the year 1812; but it was the last ray of their expiring lamp, and, whatever opinion may be formed of the principle they contended for, by the political economist, their last struggle, to save themselves from degradation, was glorious: it reflected no discredit upon those who conducted it, and drew down encomiums from the very judges who, afterwards, condemned them, as a matter of expedience.

After the failure of the application to parliament in 1811, it was determined to try the question on the existing law, which empowered magistrates to affix rates of wages. These acts had been passed in the Scots' parliament, and were confirmed by several bills, passed after the Union; the last in the reign of George II. They had been acted upon at no distant period, and a case occurred, at this time, which produced a legal opinion, that put their applicability beyond question. A cotton spinner was tried and found guilty, at the Glasgow circuit, for combination and assault arising out of a dispute about wages. The Lord Justice Clerk, (Hope, now Lord President of the Court of Session,) in passing sentence, charged it as an aggravation of the crime, that there was no necessity for combining, there being a clear remedy in law, by taking the case before the magistrates, who were legally bound to affix a reasonable rate of wages. It was therefore determined to try the experiment, but, before hazarding the expence and delay necessarily attending a litigation, as well as to endeavour to conciliate all parties, an attempt was made to bring the trade to an agreement, by an extrajudicial arrangement, which it was intended should be afterwards sanctioned by the magistrates. Here an incident occurred, which is worthy of notice, as illustrative of the little attention too frequently paid to the complaints of the labouring classes, however well founded, when made individually, and accounts for their often having recourse to collective measures. In January 1812, a deputation waited upon the Lord Provost of Glasgow, requesting him to call a meeting of the magistrates, to receive a petition and memorial from the operative weavers, praying them to exercise the powers, vested in them by law, to affix a reasonable rate of wages in the cotton manufacture. The Lord Provost scouted the idea, and would not even listen to the request, when the committee of management, for the operatives' interest, (aware that nothing but the weight of numbers would force attention to their claims,) passed a resolution, that their petition and a remonstrance should be presented, at the head of the aggregate body, and gave notice to the magistrates accordingly. This produced the desired effect. The magistrates, struck with a panic at the threat of such an assemblage, immediately intimated, that they were ready to receive their petition and memorial, if they would recall their order and present it by a deputation. This proposition being acceded to, the petition was presented, addressed to the Lord Provost, Magistrates and Sheriff of the County, and, after a long conference, it was agreed, that the magistrates should call a meeting of the trade; that two committees should be appointed, consisting of eight, for the interest of the master manufacturers and an equal number for that of the operatives, to meet and discuss the merits of the question, in presence of the magistrates of the city and county. I was appointed one of the members of the committee for the operative interest, which was the first cause of bringing me in contact with a gentleman, and led to a connexion which (whether intended by him or not) has had a powerful and injurious influence over my future destiny. Kirkman Finlay, Esq. the gentleman alluded to, was a member of the opposite committee; in extensive business, as a merchant and manufacturer; highly esteemed for his extensive commercial knowledge; at the time president of the Chamber of Commerce of Glasgow, and had been a magistrate of the city. He was perfectly conversant with all the writers on political economy, and his opinion was directly opposed to restrictions on trade or on the price of labour, under any modification; for which reason he had been appointed, as were most of the others on the same side. From 1809, I had been active in promoting the association formerly mentioned, the organization of which had been now nearly completed, and had taken a lead in the application to parliament, in 1811, which had given me a considerable degree of popularity. The committee, of which I was a member, consisted, with one or two exceptions, of practical men, acquainted only with the technicalities of their trade, and had no knowledge of the general theory upon which the arguments of our opponents were chiefly founded. The conference and debate took place in the council chamber, in the presence of upwards of twenty magistrates of the county and city. On our part, the weight of the discussion, on the abstract points, fell upon me, in reply to Mr. Finlay: and, at the close of the debate, (after paying me some marked compliments,) he requested me to call upon him, privately, at his own house, for the purpose of discussing some arguments I had brought forward, which he was not at the time prepared to answer. He said he had formed so favourable an opinion of me, that, if I would point out any way in which he could be of service, in promoting my views in life, I might fully command his interest, as he would feel great pleasure in exerting it. I replied, that I felt obliged for his good opinion, but as I appeared there as the representative of a numerous and suffering body, it was necessary for me to retain their confidence, to enable me to perform my duty and fulfil the trust they reposed in me; and, as I could not do so, were I known to have private conferences with a gentleman of his influence, who had declared himself so decidedly hostile to their claims, I must decline meeting him any where but in public, until I ceased to hold an official situation. Mr. Finlay never appeared again in the committee, and I had no farther intercourse with him until November.

Various other meetings were held, but, although many of the masters were anxious to adopt some regulation, we could come to no general agreement, either as to principle or detail; and the magistrates of the city and sheriff of the county, refusing to act, on the ground of not being competent, the attempt was abandoned. The opinion of counsel was then taken, who advised that an action should be raised before the quarter sessions, that a table of prices should be drawn up and founded upon, and as many masters made parties as would embrace a specimen of all the fabrics in the trade. Forty of the leading manufacturing houses, in Glasgow, were cited, as parties, by upwards of fifteen hundred workmen, to decide the question for Scotland; and, that no inconvenience might result from the partial operation of a decision, another action was raised, at Carlisle, to try the case in the English courts. The other counties were also in readiness to proceed, if necessary, but the whole energies were directed to the action at Glasgow, on the issue of which all the rest depended. I was one of a committee, of five, who conducted the process. The petition was presented to the justices early in March, and answers were ordered to be lodged within a few days. The defenders in the action were not agreed among themselves, but a part of them made appearance, and written pleadings followed, at considerable length. They disputed the competency of the court; the relevancy and expediency of the action, and, early in May, counsel were heard, *viva voce*, on the points at issue, before a numerous bench of magistrates. Mr. Jeffery*, who was employed for the prosecution, to obviate all objections which might be urged on the merits of the case, withdrew, *in hoc statue*, the imperative part of the prayer, when the court repelled the objection against its own competency, found the action relevant and ordered the defenders to state, specifically, in a minute, their objections to the table of rates founded upon. Against this sentence the masters appealed to the Supreme Court, by bill of advocation, where we were obliged to follow them, to obtain a decision upon the points of law†; and about the same time the ma-

* As this gentleman's name will frequently be mentioned in the subsequent part of this narrative, it is proper for me to state, that it was at this time and after giving him a detailed account of the condition of the people, employed in the cotton manufacture, to prepare him for this debate, that he expressed a desire to render me any personal service in his power, and, notwithstanding the very ambiguous situation in which public opinion has placed me, I have continued to receive the strongest proofs of his kindness and attention, in consequence of his knowledge of the real circumstances of my case.

† A collateral circumstance occurred at this time worthy of notice. Our disputes with America, on our Orders in Council, and

gistrates of the county of Cumberland gave a similar decision, in the case at Carlisle, which was also appealed, and carried, by writ of mandamus, into the Court of King's Bench. In the Scotch court, the Lord Ordinary, on the bills, ordered printed memorials, in which the case was argued ably, at great length, by both parties, and, on the 27th of June, it was decided, by the Second Division of the Court of Session, who affirmed the power of the justices of the peace to affix a rate of wages, found the action relevant and remanded the case back to the quarter sessions, to decide upon the merits. It is difficult to say what decision the Supreme Court would have given, had the merits of the case been before them; but, as the presiding judge had been a member of the committee of the House of Commons, to which the

the strict enforcement of the blockade against France and her dependencies, had risen to the greatest height, and had so completely annihilated all direct trade, that the whole commercial and manufacturing interests agreed to unite their strength, to procure a repeal of the obnoxious measure. London, Liverpool, Bristol, Manchester, &c. had presented petitions, and Mr. Brougham had commenced his brilliant parliamentary career by a motion for the repeal in the House of Commons. The gentlemen who had taken up the question, in Glasgow, had taken no steps to attract public attention to the subject, and the petition was only signed by about 200 persons, engaged in the American trade. Mr. Finlay, from an experience of the advantages to be derived from *a contraband* trade, under the licence system*, was a decided enemy to the repeal; and the town council and magistrates being a self-elected body, consisting of only thirty-two persons, he had acquired sufficient influence over them to carry a petition against the repeal by a small majority. Both petitions were presented, on the same evening, in the House of Commons, and Mr. Perceval, (then Chancellor of the Exchequer,) with his usual ingenuity, assumed, that the constituted authorities of Glasgow were to be considered as declaring the mind of the whole commercial and manufacturing interest of Scotland, which was proved by the petition attempted

* He was examined and gave evidence to that effect, before the parliamentary committee, when the encomiums passed on his extensive information and intelligence was the probable cause of stimulating him to obtain a seat in the House of Commons.

petition, for a minimum had been referred, in 1809, and had strongly imbibed the opinions then given; the probability is, that they would not have sanctioned the expediency of interfering, and, under that impression, our subsequent measures were taken.

On the case being remanded back to the justices, they ordered a proof to establish the reasonableness of the rate of wages demanded, which, brought us, at last, to the point we were so anxious to attain; but here the opposite party, in place of entering fairly into the merits and ascertaining, by a cool and dispassionate judicial investigation, what the trade could in reality afford, confined themselves to taking advantage of legal forms and technicalities to obstruct and embarrass the proceedings, and when these were, at length,

to be got up, in opposition to their views, being only signed by a few merchants, directly interested in the trade with America. The merchants of Glasgow were much reflected upon, for their supineness, by the supporters of the repeal, in England; and, in this dilemma, I was applied to, to take the necessary measures to call forth a declaration of public opinion, in the speediest manner possible. There was very little time to correct the error, as the final discussion came on in a few days; I therefore advised a public meeting of the inhabitants, to be immediately called, at which I presided, and, by the most indefatigable exertion, in five days, sent off a petition, from Lanarkshire, signed by upwards of 20,000 persons; another from Renfrewshire, by above 7000, which, with one from Leith, comprised the whole commercial and manufacturing interest.

This was decisive of the question, as it respected Scotland: the minister could no longer cavil, and a measure was repealed, which, if done a few weeks earlier, would have prevented the war with America. My correspondence with several members of parliament and other persons in the country, as chairman of the above meeting and manager of the petition, was seized among my other papers, at a subsequent period, and, although it could not be directly connected with the charge then brought against me, it made a strong impression on the minds of the crown lawyers, and had considerable influence in deciding the line of conduct I pursued.

got over, they abandoned their post and would not meet us in the proof. So deep an interest did the whole operative class feel, in this expensive and protracted litigation, that they had, almost to a man, contributed small sums, in its support; and, as we were restricted from examining persons as witnesses who had either, directly or indirectly, done so, it was with the utmost difficulty we could procure evidence. The opposite party, not having made appearance, in this stage of the proceedings, to produce any counter evidence, it may appear something like an *ex-parte* proof, but, as it is, the only judicial investigation of the kind, that ever took place in this country, I will state the manner in which it was done, for the purpose of showing the actual condition of the labouring class, in this branch of manufacture.

The witnesses were men regularly bred to the business, (women and boys not being admissable,) and were all examined upon oath. The table of rates, founded upon in the process, was assumed as the standard, and two witnesses, at least, swore to each particular fabric and the number of yards they could produce, at the rate of ten hours labour per day. The result was as follows:

	£	s.	d.
Clear weekly average wages of weavers, on all the variety of plain fabrics	0	11	11¼
Ditto, on flowered and fancy goods of all kinds,	0	15	7½
General average	0	13	9½
Minimum of the above	0	8	0
Maximum	1	0	6

The actual prices, paid for weaving at the time, were considerably *below* the above rate; and, incredible as it may appear, they were reduced to not less than 70 per cent under it at the end of 1816. As a contrast, ten other trades and professions were examined; viz. taylors, shoemakers, blacksmiths, masons, &c. which, including common labourers, produced a *general* average of 18*s*. 4½*d*. per week.

A number of master manufacturers gave evidence as to the utility of having a fixed rate of wages. Physicians and surgeons, of the first eminence, were also examined, who had inspected the workshops, and were acquainted with the diseases of the workmen, and they gave it as their decided opinion, that men could not labour in such situations more than ten hours a day, without rapidly impairing their health and producing premature decay. Upwards of 120 witnesses were examined, which occupied more than two months, the proof commencing on the 14th of August and ending on the 20th of October*.

* I shall here relate an incident, which occurred about this time, indicative of the state of public feeling, and the relation in which I stood; and, although it may not possess much general, may have some local, interest. Parliament was dissolved and the general election came on in October, at the same time that the greater part of the Scotch boroughs elect their local magistracy, and Mr. Finlay, who had been elected lord provost of Glasgow, had declared himself a candidate to represent that district of boroughs in parliament. He had publicly stated, that he started on the independent interest; but, in consequence of his known and continued opposition to the principle of affixing a rate of wages, was very unpopular among the labouring classes. He had, however, secured the town council of Glasgow in his interest, and Mr. Campbell of Blytheswood, the ministerial candidate, having Renfrew and Dumbarton, the decision rested with Rutherglen, Glasgow being the returning borough. Rutherglen is one of the few Scots boroughs that have anything like a popular election, and, out of a council of fifteen, it was possible to return seven operative weavers, and a very small effort would have procured a majority in the council. In a political point of view, the borough was divided into three parties; the majority was in the whig interest, under the influence of the house of Hamilton; a small party was attached to the tory interest, watching every opportunity to gain an ascendency; the third professed to be independent. Lord Archibald Hamilton had commenced a keen and somewhat doubtful contest for the county of Lanark, and it was understood, but not publicly avowed, that he had offered his interest, in the borough of Rutherglen, to Mr. Finlay, in exchange for the county votes he or his friends could command. The whole population were directly dependent upon the cotton manufacture, and a strong determination had been ma-

The quarter sessions appointed the 3rd of November to hear counsel finally on the merits of this important question, but the masters, who had not ventured to meet us in the proof, could not now attempt to overturn the facts we had established, by the vague and general declamation of counsel, and they left their side of the bar vacant, setting us at defiance. Mr. Jeffrey, who again appeared for the pursuers, commented, on the facts adduced in evidence,—on the advantages that would arise from a regulation which would put an end to unprincipled speculation on the price of labour, and, in a greater degree, ensure the comfort of the workmen; that the defenders had not attempted to show that the trade was not able to afford that

nifested to oppose Mr. Finlay's election, while he and his friends were making every exertion to conciliate their good opinion. A deputation had been appointed to wait upon him, to put certain queries relative to his opinions on the policy of affixing a rate of wages, and I had been solicited, by the people of Rutherglen, to attend, to put the questions; upon his answers to which depended their support. While things remained *in dubio*, one of the late magistrates of Glasgow and another gentleman, in Mr. Finlay's interest, applied to me, stating that, as my political opinons were known to be liberal, I could not but prefer Mr. Finlay to the ministerial candidate, and that such was my influence with the people of Rutherglen, that I had only to say so to them, and he would be elected! I replied, that I did not believe I had much influence in the case, at all events, none of a political kind, by which alone these matters were decided; that though, in a general point of view, I considered Mr. Finlay, from his superior knowledge and experience, the fittest of the two to represent a commercial and manfacturing district, I viewed the question as one altogether distinct from general politics; that all Mr. Finlay's influence had been exerted against a measure which involved the interest of the whole manufacturing population; and that, if it were in my power, to prevent him from extending the sphere of that influence, by a seat in parliament, I would exert it to the utmost of my ability. On the same day, a similar application was made to me, through the medium of our law-agent, by a gentleman, a friend of Mr. Campbell, and for the same purpose. I stated to him distinctly and candidly, that my political opinions differed entirely from Mr. Campbell's and his friends, and, on the ground of general politics, I would not interfere; but that I was very anxious rate: and that, even if they had done so, a branch of manufacture, which would not afford a subsistence to the people employed, had better at once be abandoned; and concluded a luminous speech by calling upon the justices to declare the rate of wages demanded reasonable. On the 10th of November the justices gave their final decision, finding the table of prices, as amended by the proof, moderate and reasonable. The difficulty now was, to bring the masters to conform to this decision, as it was perfectly understood they were determined to resist paying the rate, and the sentence of the justices, being only declaratory, no penalty could be inflicted for their paying below it. It was equally well known that, if we ap-

to prevent Mr. Finlay from getting the seat, and would do so, if in my power. The same idea seemed to be entertained here, as to the extent of my influence, and, on being informed of the grounds upon which Mr. Campbell's friends rested their hopes, I stated that I would very soon ascertain the actual state of the case, and whether or not any assitance I could give afforded a rational prospect of success, and if there were none, I should, at all events, have the means of preventing him from throwing away money upon a useless contest. I very soon got into the whole arcana of the politics of the borough, but we were too late; a few days sooner and Mr. Finlay would not have had the seat; the popular part of the election was already too far advanced, where alone my influence could have had effect. Lord Archibald Hamilton had carried the county and had operated on the whig party with a more powerful weight than either the interest of the public question, then at issue, or my oratory. The deputation met Mr. Finlay in the house of one of his friends, without *my presence* being necessary, and the arguments he used, in justification of his opposition, were *so substantial and convincing*, that he was considered by far the fittest representative! I however prevented Mr. Campbell from being deceived by a party who attempted to hold out hopes where there were none. I had never, at that time, spoken with that gentleman, but he proved his conviction of the accuracy of the information I had given, and his satisfaction with my conduct, at a subsequent period, by rendering me the most important services, when I had few friends to depend upon;—services which I can never repay but with gratitude. The view I obtained, on this occasion, into the interior of an independent Scotch borough, conveyed no very high idea of independence.

plied to the court for an imperative decree, it would be resisted, which would have forced us into another litigation; and, judging, from the sentiments expressed by the supreme court, when the case was formerly before them, the issue was more than doubtful against us. Several of the fabrics could, perhaps, not afford the price affixed by the table of rates, but the masters evinced no disposition to come forward and show what the trade could in reality enable them to pay, while some were actually at the time paying 30 per cent. more than others, for the same fabrics. The operatives, suffering, harassed, and tired out with a long litigation, were elated with their almost unexpected success, and believing they had the law upon their side, considered they were justified, in refusing to work under what that law had declared to be reasonable. It was evident too, that if the principle of working for a lower rate of wages was once given way to, it rendered nugatory all that had been done. In this state of things, with no prospect of an amicable arrangement, after consulting with our councel, we resolved to bring it to a trial of strength, in the hope we should at least be able to effect some kind of compromise. We could calculate little on a war of resources; the body of operatives was too numerous and already too poor to contend with their masters, in this respect; nor was there any rational prospect of being able to hold out until the market was empty of goods. All therefore depended upon one simultaneous moral effort, which would overawe and force their masters and the country to acknowledge the justice of their claims, and, like men conscious of the situation in which they stood, were determined to make the last stand for their rank in society*. Nor was there ever such an

* Many ridiculous opinions have been entertained on the pro-

effort made in this country. England never could have done it. Scotland could not do it now, without immediately producing riot and disturbance; fifteen years of progressive degradation have changed the character of her manufacturing population. We were not ignorant of the power assumed by the High Court of Justiciary to inflict punishment, at common law, in cases of combination; but no such case as this had ever occurred. We set up no hypothetical, unreasonable, or ideal, claim. We had the declared opinion and sanction of a court of law, after the fullest investigation, that what was demanded was only reasonable, and we scrupulously obeyed the law, courting and inviting enquiry into the justice of our demand, in every stage of the proceeding. At this time the operatives had the most unlimited confidence in the committee who had managed the process; whose influence over the body was proportionally extensive. The justices gave their decision

priety of the weavers striking work who had webs in their looms, and absurd reports circulated as to who advised that measure. The whole matter was concocted with and fully understood by our counsel, as affording the only chance of bringing about an accommodation. In putting the construction which we did upon the interlocutor of the justices, that it applied equally to the work in the hands of the workmen as to what was to be given out in future, we gained even the legal advantage; for, although we knew that their explanation would ultimately be against our construction, we protracted their decision until we had tried the effect of the experiment, and this was managed with more dexterity and address than any other part of the proceedings. The fact was, that the committee had always more difficulty in managing the body of operatives than in conducting the prosecution; and those who entertain the opinion, that it could have been better effected by the still more divided interests, which striking in detail would unquestionably have produced, only show their ignorance of mankind and of the actual condition of the operative class. For my own part, I do not shrink from the responsibility of having advised the measure, (of which I had my full share,) and, on looking back, at the distance of twelve years, I would not now act otherwise, if placed in the same circumstances.

on the 10th of November, and an ordinary meeting of delegates was held, in Glasgow, on the 12th, at which the experiment to be tried was understood, although not discussed, and full discretionary powers were given to the committee to act according to the best of their judgment. Deputies were immediately sent to inform the country districts, that it was the opinion of the committee that no work should be done, unless the price was paid, and at a meeting of delegates from nearly eighty towns and villages, held on the 18th, in presence of the procurator fiscal of the county, (who had been invited to attend,) they declared that it was the unanimous resolution of the whole body, whom they represented, not to work under the rates declared reasonable by law. On that day 20,000 looms stopped work, and, in a few days more, they were increased to near double the number; scarcely the sound of a shuttle being heard from Aberdeen to Carlisle, connected with the cotton manufacture. Every thing remained in the most profound peace; no tumult or disturbance of any kind took place, and, excepting that greater numbers were passing to and from Glasgow, it exhibited the appearance of one continued Sunday, which in Scotland, is remarkable for its stillness and placidity. The trade in England and Ireland had been apprized of what was intended, but no pecuniary assistance was either expected or received from them, nor could any fund be previously raised, that could have any influence on the subsistence of such a large body, which, including all the branches of the trade, involved not less than 200,000 persons. Every disposition was, however, shown to assist one another; the funds of friendly societies were borrowed, and joint securities given, for credits, in many various ways; but it was the impression we calculated on being able to make on opinion, not on pecuniary rescources, or physical power, to which we looked for success. Things went on, with little variation, for more than three weeks; a few fabrics were given out, at the prices affixed by the table, but no disposition had been shown to effect any general compromise, and we soon learnt the cause. All the disposable troops in Scotland were ordered to the western counties, and cantoned in the various towns and villages; and it was rumoured, that the operatives were to be put down by force. Mr. Finlay was now Member of Parliament and Lord Provost of Glasgow, and, on the rumour reaching the committee, we sent him a card, requesting an interview, which was immediately acceded to, when we stated that, as every thing had hitherto gone on peaceably, if an attempt was made to take us into custody publicly, it would exasperate the people and we could not be answerable for the consequences; that, as we were not conscious of having acted in any respect illegally, if they had any charge against us, we were ready to answer it, and would attend, at any time or place, on receiving intimation. He said he was not aware of any such intention; but were such a thing thought of, our request should be complied with; and strongly expressed his thanks for our attention to the preservation of the public peace. This promise was kept with my colleagues, but not with me; for two days afterwards, the sheriff of Renfrewshire (in which county I then resided) entered my house with a posse of officers; seized all my papers, both public and private; and, by his warrant, I was sent to the jail of Paisley, guarded by a strong detachment of cavalry. I underwent an examination of upwards of eight hours, conducted by the depute and substitute sheriffs, and, late in the evening, was liberated on bail, on my promise of attending for further examination, if required. On the following morning, proclamations, from the sheriffs and magistrates, were posted up in Glasgow, prohibiting our meetings, declaring all our proceedings illegal, and my colleagues, who had been sent for the previous day, I found in custody, remanded for further examination. A meeting of delegates, from all the districts, having been previously appointed, to take place the day after, I sent a note to the sheriff depute of Lanarkshire, requesting his attendance, to state the grounds upon which he had declared our proceedings illegal. In consequence of this intimation, he accompanied me to the meeting, attended by his officers, when he ordered it immediately to disperse, declaring it to be illegal, without assigning any other reason for his conduct, than that he would take the responsibility upon himself. We informed him, that, as it was our opinion we were protected by the constitution, and were acting agreeably to law, we would not disperse, unless compelled by force, when he ordered his officers to take the president out of the chair and the meeting quietly dissolved.

The sheriff, on this occasion, informed me, that he had been applied to by a number of the most respectable manufacturing houses, who had expressed a wish for an accommodation, but that they considered a number of the fabrics were higher rated than the trade would afford them to pay.

I replied, that the operatives had, perhaps, been in the first instance, a little elevated with their success, and many of them, not being capable of taking a very comprehensive view of their own relative situation, or of the state of the trade generally, would make no concession from the rates affixed by the justices; but now, since they had felt their own weight, I had no doubt but some reduction would be cheerfully submitted to, on reasons being adduced and the arrangement sanctioned by the magistrates,—at all events, that the committee were ready to receive any proposition for a compromise, and would use their influence to get the operative body to agree. We never, however, heard more upon the subject; the interference of government soon enabled the masters to discover, that they had only to hold off a little longer, and the operatives would be obliged to submit at discretion.

In a day or two after, my colleagues being admitted to bail, I went to Edinburgh, to take the opinion of counsel on the legality of the proceedings of the magistrates; but there I learned, that the question would be immediately tried by the crown lawyers instituting criminal proceedings against us. The justices now gave their judgment, that they did not intend their interlocutor to apply to previous engagements; and, in compliance with their decision, those who had work on hand immediately began to finish it. For a considerable time, however, no more was taken out, but it was easy to perceive, from that period, that the question was finally lost. The situation of the committee became most arduous and difficult, many of the operatives foreseeing what was approaching, conceived themselves treated with flagrant injustice, to be thus crushed by the mere influence of force, and disappointed, irritated, and nearly actuated by despair, were for having recourse to stronger measures, and with difficulty could be restrained from violence. We were accused by many for the paucity of our proceedings and want of energy, in not calling into action the whole body in England and Ireland, to obtain, by force, what the law had declared we were entitled to*. Meetings of delegates continued to be held privately: these we still attended, and, notwithstanding the criminal prosecutions pending over our heads, did not abandon our post. We impressed, upon the minds of the more reflecting, the impropriety of having recourse to violence or coercion; and employed them in all directions, to counteract the intentions of those differently disposed. This influence we continued to exercise, until, one district giving way after another, the contest was finally given up about the end of February, 1813, having continued nine weeks; half of which time, the whole looms, engaged in the cotton manufacture in Scotland, (with a few

* Attempts were repeatedly made, during the year 1812, to introduce the Luddite organization into Scotland, from the manufacturing counties in England; and we were both individually tampered with, and directly applied to, in our official capacity, for that purpose. They asserted we never would obtain redress by our legal proceedings; and that nothing would accomplish the purpose but a general destruction of all the machinery introduced, to abridge human labour; but we steadily resisted all their attempts, and carefully concealed from the operatives that ever they were made. It is now well known, that Buonaparte calculated upon his continental system producing insurrections in our manufacturing districts, and there is hardly a doubt that he had emissaries employed in this country, for the purpose of fomenting them. I was introduced to a person, in Lancashire, in the spring of 1813, who was deeply implicated in those measures; he knew the channels through which the overtures had been made to us; had been twice tried, but was fortunate enough to escape conviction, and he informed me, that money had been frequently liberally distributed, and that he had, at different times, himself received considerable sums. We were also suspected of having a correspondence with the militia, who were at that time contending for the right of being discharged after a certain period of service. The only foundation for this suspicion was, that the committees of one or two of the regiments applied to us, for instructions as to the form of drawing up petitions to be presented to the Prince Regent. Had we been inclined, we could easily have extended a connexion with the regiments belonging to the manufacturing counties; but we had no such purpose in view, although, from that impression, some of the troops were removed to England, and replaced by others.

trifling exceptions,) were at a stand. As, in all cases of generalship, it required greater skill to cover the retreat than to lead them into the field, and although a good deal depended upon those who managed it, the propriety of conduct evinced in this arduous contest was mainly attributable to the general good sense prevailing among the body of operatives of Scotland; for, without intending any thing invidious to the inhabitants of the sister kingdom, I must say, that the party we found the greatest difficulty in restraining, were chiefly emigrants from that country. There was not, however, a single personal assault committed, nor property destroyed, with the exception of a few panes of glass broken, and some trifling injury done to a few webs in the looms; and it is very doubtful whether these were not committed by persons inimical to the business, for the purpose of throwing a slur upon our proceedings. At all events, five pounds would have covered all the damages sustained. The distance from the seat of government, and the peaceable manner in which it was conducted, made this affair be comparatively little attended to, although it is the most singular moral phenomenon in the history of our manufacturing population.

Having now given a general view of the proceedings in this very curious case, it is necessary for me to advert to my individual situation, during the latter part of the contest; and as it only serves to illustrate individual character, upon which every one is at liberty to form his opinion, I will offer no comment, but distinctly call upon the parties, should an attempt be made to contravert or invalidate my statement.

I formerly mentioned, that I had no personal intercourse with Mr. Finlay, from the time he appeared as a member of the opposite committee, in

January, until November. When we formed the determination of striking work, on the decision of the justices being given in our favour, on the 10th of the latter month, I visited the most important districts, to prepare them for the approaching event, and did not return to Glasgow until the 18th, the day appointed for carrying it into execution. Rumours of our intention having been circulated, excited considerable alarm in the minds of the magistracy. Mr. Finlay, during my absence, had caused repeated inquiries to be made after me, and, immediately on my arrival, a person, sent by him, waited upon me with a very pressing request to see me without delay. I communicated this to one of my colleagues, and on considering the great extent of Mr. Finlay's influence, and the vast importance it was to us, at so critical and dangerous a moment, to impress upon his mind the justice and expediency of effecting some arrangement, we together called upon him, at his own house, after the business of the day was finished. A number of the arguments for and against the expediency of restrictions on the price of labour were gone over, without making much impression on either side; we informed him of our determination, and, at parting, he requested to see me alone, in a day or two, to discuss the subject at greater length. Several interviews followed, when all the arguments of Smith, Malthus, and the economists of the French school, that were applicable to the general principle, were discussed; and, not coming to any agreement upon the point at issue, he made a direct attack upon my personal situation. He said that, in a personal point of view, it was a matter of no moment to me what became of the question; that *my own talents would command friends,* sufficient to insure my advancement in life; and that, if I would exert myself, to make the operatives give up the contest and return to their work, or even withdraw my support from them, an *independent* and *permanent* provision should be made for me, in any manner I wished or chose to point out. I replied, that I had never taken up the question as a personal one, but as one involving the interest of the whole population employed in the cotton manufacture, and eventually that of the whole community; that I had acted from conscientious motives, believing the claim to be legal, just, and even expedient; and that, although the conduct pursued by the operatives did not depend upon my exertions alone, whatever influence I possessed should be exerted in their support, as long as a shadow of success remained.

After I had been held to bail, and the operatives were beginning to waver, he pressed the same argument, urging that it was now evident we could not succeed; and that, to save myself and put an end to it at once, I should follow his advice, when I stated that, even admitting the result to be as he predicted, the peace of the country and the safety of the operatives would more than ever require my exertion, to prevent them from rushing into error.

When the result became obvious, the night previous to Mr. Finlay going to take his seat in parliament, he again requested to see me. He said he now called upon me for the last time; that indictments would immediately be preferred against us, before the High Court of Justiciary, and that, as I was looked upon as the principal leader, the severest punishment awaited me; that the papers, containing the final instructions and information for the crown lawyers to proceed, were that night to be sent to Edinburgh; but if I would act as he had desired, *my* trial would not be proceeded with, and I might have any terms I wished otherwise. I told him I believed his own influence had contributed largely to prevent any accommodation; but, although I was now afraid we were not likely to succeed, if the men who had hitherto held the confidence of the well-disposed part of the operative body were to abandon them, a party would succeed to the management, ready to go any length; and as the feelings of the people were irritated by disappointment and their passions wrought up to the highest pitch, the greatest excesses and outrages might be committed, which could only terminate in their own destruction. With this conviction on my mind, I considered it would be in the highest degree dastardly and cowardly to desert them for any personal consideration. He replied, that, by persisting in that line of conduct, I would ruin my family and my prospects in life; that I was much more blameable than those who had acted from ignorance, as I was capable of taking a more enlarged view of the subject, and therefore more culpable, and my punishment would consequently be more severe; that there was no probability of my being allowed to remain in the country, but that he should be happy if he had it inhis power to render any assistance to my family, or me, at any future time. I finally answered, that if, as he alleged, I had been the chief instrument in leading on the operatives, it was my imperative duty to endeavour to bring them off; that my honour and sincerity were both committed, and I would not desert them at that crisis, if all my hopes and prospects should perish. Here the interview terminated, and I have been thus circumstantial in the detail, that it may be contrasted with events which follow; and have no other observation to make, but that it is true to the *very letter*.

In a few days after, criminal indictments were preferred against us, to stand trial before the High Court of Justiciary, for combination and conspiracy. There was no statute law upon which we could be tried, or that affixed any specific punishment for this crime, nor had any case of the same nature ever come before that court. We had acted on the decision given by a bench of magistrates, and consonant with the opinion of the highest criminal judge in the kingdom; but the Court of Justiciary were struck with a panic at the formidable extent and perfection of our organization, and were determined, at all events, to put it down. That court possesses, at common law, legislative as well as judicial powers, to which it can give a retrospective as well as a prospective effect, to meet any new case that may arise, but had they possessed an accurate knowledge of the actual condition and feelings of the population, (putting aside the palpable violation of justice and taking it merely as a matter of expedience,) they would have seen it was quite unnecessary to inflict personal punishment. The bulk of mankind never bear in mind that, although it is not in mortals to command success, they may do more; they may deserve it. He that engages in the popular cause must expect his efforts to be estimated by eventual success, not the motive and means he has taken to attain it; if he acts conscientiously, he will find himself one day idolized, carried on their shoulders and treated like a demigod; and the next, trampled in the mire and bespattered with mud, when he is least conscious of deserving it. So it was in this instance; the operatives had made their last effort; their last round of ammunition was expended, without producing the desired effect; and, incapable of proper discrimination, when they found themselves disappointed, the bulk of them were ready to turn round upon the men who had sacrificed everything in their defence. The organization had fallen to pieces, and no effort could have kept them together; and, to prevent the recurrence of any thing similar, it was only necessary for the court to declare the law.

Besides the committee, there were several others, who had filled subordinate situations, indicted, and, on receiving mine, I went to Edinburgh to consult with Messrs. Jeffrey and Cockburn, our counsel, who endeavoured to ascertain what view the crown lawyers and the court entertained. They soon learnt that the necessity of making a severe example had made so deep an impression on their minds, that nothing short of transportation was contemplated; that there was no hope of being able to remove that impression at the time; and, under those circumstances, they decidely advised that none of the parties, who had taken a lead, should hazard standing trial, but forfeit their recognizances and leave the kingdom. This was particularly insisted on in my case, for reasons already explained, and, after considerable hesitation, I very reluctantly complied. I returned to Glasgow, communicated my determination to my colleagues, and gave all the assistance in my power in the measures necessary for the defence of those who were to appear, until the day prior to the trial.

This trial took place before the High Court of Justiciary, on the 9th of March, 1813, and excited great interest. The crown lawyers attempted to prove that overt acts of violence and intimidation had arisen out of the combination, but utterly failed in showing they had been committed, or even countenanced, by any of the parties indicted, the very reverse being clearly established; so that, admitting the decision of the quarter sessions, upon which we proceeded, to have had no force, (which, in the eye of justice, was absurd,) the only charge substantiated was, simple combination. On the analogy of the English statutes, the Court of Justiciary had, a short time before, declared simple combination a crime punishable at common law, although no conviction had previously taken place. This power, however, when assumed by that court, was very different in its consequences from the English statute law, which was considered oppressive, although it restricted the punishment to three months imprisonment, while the Scotch court might give a month's imprisonment, or transportation for life at discretion, having no check in such cases but public opinion. Mr. Jeffrey and Mr. Cockburn conducted the defence with an energy and ability seldom equalled in the profession, and which they could not have surpassed, had they been personally interested. In vain, however, did they urge that, after the judgment of the court below, the operatives were justified in striking work, had contravened no law, and were therefore guilty of no crime. By the construction put upon it by the court, the jury returned a verdict of guilty, and various periods of imprisonment, from four to eighteen months, were inflicted upon them that were present, and sentence of outlawry was passed against those who were absent. The court declared the sentences were much more lenient than they originally intended, pronounced the association which had been recommended by different members of parliament illegal, and prohibited the payment of all debts contracted in its support*. On this judgment being given in the Scotch court, the case at

* The crown lawyers on the trial denied all previous knowledge of the existence of the association, although the Lord Advocate had been furnished with copies of the articles in the beginning of 1810. In 1811, an investigation had also taken place by the sheriffs of the counties of Renfrew and Lanark, when they got

Carlisle was abandoned, and in the ensuing session of parliament, the late Marquis of Londonderry brought in a bill to repeal the acts upon which we had founded the action, and were then suffering exile and imprisonment for obeying.

To get out of the jurisdiction of the court, I proceeded to Lancashire, where I had only remained a short time, when proclamations were published, offering a reward for my apprehension. I however received information, in sufficient time, to enable me to proceed to Dublin, in the neighbourhood of which I remained until near the end of the year. At the suggestion of several gentlemen of respectability, in Glasgow, I then returned privately to Scotland. Things having resumed their former course, as the proceedings came to be more coolly considered and better understood, their injustice became apparent, and it was the opinion of those gentlemen, that it only required a proper representation to the crown lawyers to get the sentence of outlawry rescinded. They also considered Mr. Finlay, from his official rank and influence, as well as from the opinion he had professed to them to entertain respecting me, the fittest person to make the representation, which they would second, if necessary. In this, however, we were disappointed, for, in answer to my application, he informed me, that he considered me highly culpable for acting as I had done, but more particularly for neglecting my own interest; and, as he did not think I had undergone *sufficient punishment,* he must decline all interference. Farther explanations followed, both by myself and the gentlemen interested on my account; but

possession of the books, containing the regulations and minutes of all the proceedings. The books had only been returned a few months previous to the trials, when they declared themselves perfectly satisfied; and, not anticipating a barefaced denial of so palpable a fact, we were not prepared with evidence to prove it.

all I was able to obtain, at the end of several months, was, a kind of general assurance that, if I would keep myself private and not interfere in public matters, no proceedings would be taken against me. During all this time I was separated from my family, being only able to visit them secretly; treated with ingratitude by those for whose interest I had suffered*; harassed and worn out by anxiety of mind; ruined by the expense I was subjected to, in removing from place to place; my health sunk under it, and I was confined to bed for several months. I recovered a little in the summer of 1814, and, finding I could get into no situation in business, with the sentence of outlawry suspended over my head, and Mr. Finlay showing no disposition to interest himself farther, I applied to Mr. Campbell of Blythes-wood. This gentleman was a relative of the late Archibald Colquhoun, Esq. then Lord Advocate, and afterwards Lord Register of Scotland. He had no personal knowledge of me, he only knew me by my conduct in the election at Rutherglen, in 1812; but, the moment I explained to him the nature of my situation, he zealously espoused my interest, and persevered with a degree of devoted attention seldom to be found in men of his rank in life. He explained the whole of my conduct and situation to the Lord Advocate, who did not

* It is nothing new in the history of unsuccessful popular measures, but little to the credit of the body of operatives, that they not only made no compensation to the men who had devoted their time and talents to promote their interests, but they actually left the committee incumbered with debt to a considerable amount, for law expenses. There were, no doubt, many honourable exceptions to this want of feeling, but the bulk of them evinced the most sordid apathy and indifference to their fate. One shilling each, from so large a body, would have placed the committee independent of all pecuniary embarrassments, yet that pitiful pittance was not forthcoming: a striking contrast, when compared with the sacrifices made by the operatives in many other professions.

conceive it necessary that I should undergo *farther punishment, to defecate me from individual delinquency;* he was rather anxious I should suffer no more; but there were many difficulties in the way, arising from some cases of combination, which occurred at the time, and although they were of a different nature, it made the Lord Advocate doubtful how far it would be prudent to reagitate my case, when no further punishment was intended. Several delays took place, in consequence, until my patience was completely exhausted, and I surrendered myself to the Sheriff of Renfrewshire, in March 1815, with the determination of forcing it to a conclusion. Although this step was not in accordance with the wish of the Lord Advocate, nor agreeable to Mr. Campbell's advice, (both requesting me to delay,) it had no tendency to relax his exertions, and he was indefatigable in urging the Lord Advocate to make my imprisonment as short as possible. Various causes, however, prevented me from getting reponed against the sentence of outlawry until the beginning of June, when I was admitted to bail, and served with an indictment, to stand trial before the High Court of Justiciary, on the 26th of the same month. Mr. Campbell, Mr. Cockburn, and Mr. Vans* made all the necessary arrangements, to enable me to meet the case in the most respectable manner; but the trial was not proceeded with. The court had decided the law in 1813; it was therefore agreed that I should plead guilty to the major proposition of the indictment,

* Henry S. Vans, Esq. advocate, nephew of General Dunlop. My case was introduced to this gentleman's notice by Mrs. Dunlop, the correspondent and patron of Burns, with whom I had a relative long resident. In conjunction with Mr. Jeffrey and Mr. Cockburn, he subsequently took a very warm interest in my affairs, of which I am so sensible, that any expression of thanks can convey but a faint emblem of my feelings.

with which they were satisfied; and, having produced evidence as to personal character, Mr. Cockburn made a very forcible appeal to the feelings of the court, on the extreme hardship of my case, when I received sentence of one month's additional imprisonment. The judges were not now so much under the influence of terror and alarm, and, in giving their opinions, they admitted the singularity of the case, said that no moral guilt could be imputed to me, and expressed themselves highly satisfied with my general conduct and character; but, as a matter of political expedience, they considered it their duty to put down all such attempts*.

I had suffered so much from anxiety of mind, aggravated by confinement, that my health was seriously impaired, but my friends did everything to render me comfortable during the remainder of my imprisonment; and, when it expired, evinced the greatest solicitude to assist me to get into business. It was sometime, however, before I could come to a determination, and while I remained in suspense, Mr. Jeffrey and Mr. Cockburn, relying on Mr. Finlay's former promises, suggested the propriety of me calling upon him for his advice and assistance. I accordingly wrote to him, explaining my views and wishes, and afterwards called upon him personally. He received me very coldly, said that he found no persons who would

* It was my intention to have had this publication ready for the press prior to the commencement of the last session of parliament, one object being, to attract attention to the nature and exercise of the powers assumed by the Court of Justiciary in Scotland, in cases of combination. On finding that various unexpected causes of delay would prevent me from having it ready in sufficient time, I sent that part of the manuscript to Mr. Hume, and I have the satisfaction of believing that the exposure made by its production, and my examination by the Artisans Committee, in some degree contributed towards the abrogation of the unjust and oppressive laws against combination.

allow themselves to conquer the prejudices they had imbibed against me from the manner I had acted, in the question respecting the price of manufacturing labour, and he could therefore render me no assistance. In a short time I resolved to try the experiment of a commission warehouse, in the sale of silk and cotton goods, to which I afterwards added the manufacturing of both, upon a small scale. The general peace had been a short time concluded, and, in the view of many, the prospects in business were flattering; but, being suspicious of the approaching storm, which soon after overwhelmed the commercial world, I resolved to proceed with caution. I communicated my plan and opinion to my friends, which met their approbation; and, in the spring of 1816, Mr. Jeffrey, Mr. Cockburn, and Mr. Vans, with some of their friends, who had no personal knowledge of me, made the necessary advances, to enable me to commence. Mr. Campbell at the same time offered his assistance, but, by the plan I had laid down, it was not at that time required. These gentlemen had few friends connected with commerce, but the few which they had, they endeavoured to interest in my favour. I was also promised the support of several houses, extensively engaged in the American trade, none of whom, however, had it in their power to give me a single order, the market of that country being completely glutted, almost as soon as the ports were opened. I had, in consequence, to depend in a great measure upon my own exertions, to find out other channels; and although the times were very unpropitious, and I was so unfortunate as to make bad debts to a considerable amount, soon after my commencement, I succeeded beyond my expectation. I conducted my business on a scale calculated to enable me to form an opinion of what might be done by perseverance and attention, and exposed nothing to hazard by uncertain speculation, confining my views, in the first instance, merely to cover expenses. Mr. Jeffrey being in Glasgow at the circuit, I had a long conference with him, when, in mentioning some persons who he thought might be serviceable to me, he again alluded to Mr. Finlay, and the influence he possessed in the commercial world. I told him I was perfectly aware of the benefit to be derived from any opinion which Mr. Finlay's extensive experience enabled him to give, but I would not solicit a personal favour from him. When Mr. Jeffrey replied, he should have an opportunity of seeing him soon, when he would endeavour to remove the illiberal prejudice which he seemed to have imbibed. The greatest confidence was placed in my own judgment by my friends, and it was agreed, before embarking to any considerable extent, I should, about the end of the year, give them my opinion of the probable prospects. Accordingly, on the 3d of December, I sent Mr. Jeffrey a detailed statement of my progress and situation, in which I entered fully into the view I entertained of the general state of business, and condition of the manufacturing districts. I informed him I had every rational prospect of being able to make my business respectable, and could then extend it with a greater degree of safety; but the principle upon which trade had come to be conducted, being little better than a species of gambling, some degree of uncertainty must always attend it; and as I had no hope of the system improving, it was possible, even after making every exertion, I might ultimately fail. That, were my friends to advance the necessary capital, to enable me to extend my business, and it be attended with such consequences, I could never forgive myself, if I in any way involved them, or brought them into difficulties. For these reasons, if I could procure a situation, to take the management of the business of a house, sufficiently respectable to afford a liberal salary, I should prefer it, until a more auspicious period; but, in the event of it being considered better to prosecute my own, I should prefer a security for a cash account, in a bank, to a farther advance of money. On the 8th of December I had an answer from Mr. Jeffrey, acquainting me, that he and Mr. Cockburn had read over and considered my statement. He requested me to give them an account of the practice of the banks, in giving such credits, and the amount I should require; that Mr. Cockburn had just written to Mr. Campbell, to join them in the measure, and he had no doubt but I would be accommodated to any reasonable extent; that he had that day written to Mr. Finlay and Mr. Monteith*, in very pressing terms, upon the former of whom he wished me to call, as early as possible, to acquaint him distinctly with my own views, and ascertain his opinion. Agreeable to this request, I called upon Mr. Finlay, a day or two after, and I will not pretend to say he was influenced by the feelings of Sir Giles Overreach, when addressing Wellborn,

> "We worldly men, when we see friends and kinsmen
> Past hope, sunk in their fortunes, lend no hand
> To lift them up, but rather set our feet
> Upon their heads, to press them to the bottom;
> But now I see you in a way to rise,
> I can and will assist you;"

but he now received me in a very flattering manner. He entered into all the minutiæ of my business, and, fully coinciding with me in opinion, on the general aspect of the times, thought it would be more advisable for me to obtain some respectable situation,

* Henry Monteith, Esq. then Lord Provost of Glasgow, and at present member of parliament for the Lanark district of burghs.

such as my abilities and perseverance enabled me to fill; and, to procure which, he was ready to lend all the assistance in his power. In the course of conversation, on the condition of our manufacturing establishments compared with those on the continent, an allusion was made to Mr. Owen of New Lanark. It immediately occurred to him, that a charge in that gentleman's establishment would be a desirable thing for me, and that *my information and experience* would also be an acquisition to him. Mr. Owen was then in Glasgow, and was to breakfast with Mr. Finlay next morning, and, having made an arrangement for that purpose, I attended at the same time, and was introduced to him. Mr. Finlay soon left us alone, and we spent several hours together. He gave me a detail of what he had done, and the plans he had in contemplation, which were soon after brought more prominently before the public, and I gave him an epitome of my history and opinions, and the situation in which I was then placed. Mr. Owen said he had long been in search of a person, such as he considered me to be, to superintend and assist in maturing the improvements he had begun; but, before entering into any specific agreement, he wished me to spend a few days with him at New Lanark, that I might be able to form an opinion of the progress he had already made; and it was agreed I should make my visit in a few days. Previous to Mr. Finlay leaving us, in the morning, he requested me not to leave his house until his return, as he was anxious to have some particular conversation with me, after my interview with Mr. Owen had terminated. As the communication he then made produced the most serious consequences to me, and involved matters of no slight public interest, I shall make no apology for the particularity of the long personal detail which I have given. For my own justification, it is necessary that I should state, distinctly, the precise circumstances in which I was placed; the opinions formed of me, and the estimation in which I was held, at that particular period. I may be accused of egotism; but I value not the charge: I have been immolated on the altar of prejudice, my reputation has been wounded by charges which I have not merited, and I have experienced all the dishonour of guilt, without its turpitude. I do not undervalue tbe good opinion of the world; it is necessary to happiness; but, in enquiring into my actions and judging of my motives, it may have been deceived; nor, until it is capable of forming a judgment without prejudice or bias, will I bow to its dictum and acknowledge its infallibility. I have been charged with acting from the basest and most sordid motives; but, while my conscience does not accuse me, I will indignantly repel the imputation, whether made by the sycophantic court parasite, or the unprincipled political demagogue, who ministers and panders to the appetite of the multitude. I am not ignorant how difficult it is for an obscure individual to defend his reputation against the attacks of party rage and party feeling, but I will not be deterred from the attempt, although those who had leisure to libel and accuse, should not have a minute to hear my defence, or candour to retract, where they have been wrong. The concatenation of events, which I relate, being nearly a piece of auto-biography, it is possible I may mistake, and consequently misstate, some parts of my character; self love may make me practise self deception, and prevent me from penetrating deeper than the surface, in the relation I may give, or the judgment I may form of my motives; but an intentional or unintentional perversion of facts will carry with it its own corrective and antidote; for, with a single exception, the parties are all alive, which will constitute a pretty fair standard of adjustment, and to the tribunal of public opinion I fearlessly make my appeal.

To give an idea of the state of the manufacturing districts and, before proceeding with my personal narrative, it will be necessary to take a retrospective view of public events, for sometime previous to the end of the year 1816. Our seclusion from the continent, under the operation of Buonaparte's prohibitory system, had exhausted it of British manufactures, and the partial openings, effected by his reverses in the campaign against Russia, produced a brisk demand for all kinds of British goods; the hopes of our merchants and manufacturers were highly elated, and without considering that countries, so long ravaged and impoverished by oppressions and wars of unparalleled extent and duration, could have no equivalents to give, they imagined, that, if we could only get rid of the illegitimate Usurper, the consumption and demand for British produce and manufactures would be inexhaustable. Speculations and consignments, to a vast extent, were made to every accessible part of the continent, and, for a time, every thing seemed to go on well. No sooner, however, was the fate of that extraordinary man sealed for ever; ere yet the grass grew upon the graves of our countrymen, who had fallen to restore Europe to the fostering and parental care of legitimate thrones; and while yet the sound of the blood-stained laurels of Waterloo was reverberating from one end of the empire to the other; our merchants were bankrupts; our artizans and mechanics were starving and betraying an ignorant impatience of the misery they were suffering. The hopes entertained, on the opening of the American ports, in the beginning of 1816, proved equally fallacious; and, in the summer of that year, the distress had become so great, that a general outcry was raised for the reduction of the public burdens. Many attributed a great part of the evils we were suffering to the defects in our system of national representation, and almost all, who were friendly to reform, considered it a favourable opportunity for agitating the question, when we were at profound peace with all the world. Scotland had her full share of the calamity and distress, and participated in the discontents arising out of them; while the absence of all popular representation made the theoretical errors of her political institutions more palpable and open to the attacks of those who considered the evil to have its origin in that scource. Glasgow, the focus of manufactures and of misery, as might be expected, took the lead in agitating the question; a committee was formed and an application made to the magistrates, to grant the liberty of the town hall, to hold a public meeting, to petition the throne and both houses of parliament, for retrenchment and reform. This application was peremptorily refused; and a similar one, made for liberty to meet in the public green, met with no better success. This opposition on the part of the magistrates, to say the least of it, was very unwise. Hitherto, large popular meetings, for political purposes, were almost unknown in Scotland; but this attempt to deprive the people of the very right of making their complaint and declaring their opinion, exasperated them to the highest degree and produced a general popular ferment. Official robes are not always found to cover the highest attainments, and, like the veiled prophet of Khorassan, the influence of the wearers frequently depend more upon the power they have of concealing them from the gaze of vulgar eyes, than on intellectual superiority. Accordingly, the persons, who held the discussions with the magistrates, on that occasion, did not find them capable of taking the clearest of all possible views of civil rights, nor possessing a very accurate knowledge of the condition and feelings of the people. These circumstances were made public and comparisons drawn, little to the advantage of the rulers. Squibs and dramatic pasquinades were printed and published, which produced such an effervescence of feeling among the labouring classes, that all respect for authority and subordination was lost; treated with contempt and turned into ridicule. About the same time a correspondence took place with the advocates for reform in various parts of the country, and it was suggested, by Major Cartwright and some other members of the Hampden Club, that, to obviate the objection, that the reformers were never agreed among themselves upon any specific plan, it was desirable that all minor differences of opinion should be set a side, and that the prayers of the petitions to be presented should be as near as possible uniform.

The opposition of the magistrates had a direct tendency to stimulate to greater exertions. A field was procured, in the vicinity of Glasgow, and, on the 29th of October, a meeting was held, which was attended by upwards of 40,000 persons. There, the conduct of the magistrates was freely animadverted upon and the idea conveyed, by such an assemblage, operated upon the imaginations of the people, like a shock of electricity; inducing them to believe there was no limit to their power and importance; and resolutions, in favour of retrenchment and reform, were carried by unanimous acclamation. From the time that our ancestors had opposed the arbitrary proceedings of the Stuarts, under the banner of the covenant, no such determined spirit of resistance had been manifested in Scotland; the meeting was the largest that ever had assembled, for any political purpose, and was the prelude to those which afterwards took place, that assumed a very different complexion. Had the magistrates possessed a little more knowledge of human nature, and been aware of the consequences which will invariably follow the line of conduct they adopted; had they expressed a little more sympathy and commiseration for the sufferings of the people, and freely granted a place of meeting within doors, it would have confined the proceedings to a different class, and no such result would have followed; but, as the magistrates acted in a similar manner, in many other parts of the country, the people fell into the hands of a set of illiterate and unprincipled demagogues, and were precipitated into measures that served as a pretext for abridging our general liberties. In Glasgow and neighbourhood, the condition of the great mass of the labouring population was indeed truly deplorable; many thousands were altogether out of employment, and speculation on the price of labour was carried to such an unprecedented and unprincipled extent, that those who were employed, if they had families, could not, with the utmost exertion, command as much, even of the very lowest garbage, as support life. Reckless, hopeless and desperate, they considered no change, not even anarchy itself, could render their condition worse.

At a time like this, when the sufferings of the people should have united all parties, to devise remedies to mitigate the evil, from whatever cause it proceeded, the periodical press exercised the most baneful influence over their minds. It is unnecessary and uncalled for, to name the writers who took the lead in this pernicious warfare; but, next to positive suffering, are we indebted to them for the abridgment of our liberties, the disgusting exhibition of dungeons, chains and gibbets, and for unsheathing the sabres of Englishmen upon their own deluded countrymen. The abolition of the whole civil list would have been but as a drop in the bucket, in relieving distress so generally felt; but the writers who had most influence with the labouring classes, and who were, in fact, almost the only ones read by them, artfully and ably seized upon and exposed every defect in the system of government, attributed all their sufferings to useless sinecures and pensions; taught them to look to an abstract and untried theory as a panacea for all the misery they endured; which would, in one day, sweep away all the evils that had accumulated for centuries. The whole of their reasoning, if reasoning it might be called, was addressed to the passions and not the judgment. Rank, and everything previously held sacred and venerable, was laughed at to scorn; the minds of the people were completely inflamed; a line of demarcation was drawn between the different ranks of society, and a rooted antipathy and ferocious spirit of retaliation was engendered in the minds of the labouring classes. Nor were the writers in support of the ministry less culpable; right or wrong, every measure was justified; the sufferings of the people were either altogether denied, or acknowledged to exist to a very limited extent; their murmurings and complaints were attributed to factious and unnecessary discontent; the whole vocabulary of Billingsgate was ransacked, for epithets to insult them and cover them with reproaches, and their poverty was charged against them as a crime, and constituted the very head and front of their offending. Such a state of things could not continue without coming to a crisis. The first Spafield meeting was held on the 18th of November, and the next, on the 2d of December, proceeded to open riot; the commotions in the metropolis reacted upon the country, and the whole of the manufacturing districts were thrown into a state of agitation. My situation afforded every opportunity for making observations; my business brought me in daily contact with people of all classes and opinions. I had an opportunity of knowing the situation of the merchant and master manufacturer, and the miserable condition to which the labourer was reduced. There was not a manufacturing town or village, in Scotland, with the situation of which I was not acquainted, and few where I had not some direct correspondence. As early as the month of June, 1816, conscious of what was approaching, I published letters in one of the Glasgow newspapers, pointing out the necessity of the higher classes making provision to relieve the distresses of the labouring population, before the approaching winter should drive them to desperation. Scotland, having no regular poors rate, rendered such a measure essential, and was preferable to enforcing parochial assessments; but the amount of the distress was not credited, and no steps were taken to alleviate it, until what I had predicted had actually taken place. As to my opinions on reform, I was a friend to the extension of the elective franchise; but time and experience had taught me moderation, and having previously suffered in the popular cause, I neither considered it prudent, nor felt any disposition, to take a lead in that question. My name was, however, upon the list of the committee, and I was personally acquainted and in habits of daily intercourse with the gentlemen who were active in conducting the petition from the city of Glasgow. Alexander M'Conochy, Esq. now Lord Meadowbank, was Lord Advocate, and the late James Wedderburn, Esq. Solicitor General for Scotland. These two officers, but more immediately the former, have the sheriffs of counties under their control and are responsible for the preservation of the public peace. Being but lately appointed to office, they had very little experience, and no very high opinion was entertained of their capability, either by the ministry or the local magistracy. Robert Hamilton, Esq. Sheriff Depute of the county of Lanark, had a good disposition, but was in bad health; and did not possess the general qualifications and activity to be efficient in such a situation, particularly in difficult times; and the Lord Provost for the time being, with the whole Magistrates of Glasgow, was equally inefficient. Mr. Finlay continued to occupy a seat in the House of Commons: all the magistrates looked up to him and were under his influence. He filled no official civil situation, but, in consequence of the general imbecility, in conjunction with J. Reddie, Esq. advocate, assessor for the city, he had, *de facto*, the whole local government; and, in addition to the regular channel of communication with the law officers of the crown, corresponded directly with Lord Sidmouth, the Home Secretary of State. Such was the state of the country and my situation at the end of 1816.

On again meeting Mr. Finlay, I recounted what had passed with Mr. Owen, and, on my business being disposed of, he directly adverted to the state of public affairs. He was not ignorant of my opinions and connexions, and I entered generally into the view I entertained of the existing state of things, acquainting him with the wretched condition of the people; the number I believed to be out of employment, (which, in Glasgow and its suburbs, was little short of 10,000,) and the miserable pittance paid to them that were employed*; that the people, who were actually star-

* As a statement of the relative prices of labour will convey a more correct idea of the condition of the people than general description, I shall specify the price of weaving for a few of the staple articles, in the light branch of the cotton manufacture, which requires a superior class of workmen, extracted from my books at random. I contrast the price proved as necessary to produce the average metioned in page 23, (taken in 1812, but not generally in operation later than 1809,) with that paid at the end of 1816.

Reed. *TABLE of* 1812.	*per ell.*	*Paid in* 1816.
1400 four quarter, Jaconet	9½d.	.... 3d.
Ditto six quarter, ditto	13½	.... 4½
Ditto four quarter, lawn ground...	11⅝	.... 4½
Ditto six quarter, ditto	16½	 6
1300 four quarter, gauze	16	 6
600 ditto ditto, whip net	13½	.... 2½
Ditto ditto ditto, patent ditto ...	36	 5

Wheat was oscillating between 90s. and 100s. per quarter; quartern loaf 1s. 6d.; oatmeal per peck, 1s. 10d. to 2s.; all other articles of provision, house rent, &c. at war prices. Various causes had certainly limited the demand for manufactured goods, but production was not diminished nearly on an equal ratio with the number of hands thrown out of employment, physical exhaustion being the only limit to the exertion of those employed, till their utmost efforts could not command an existence, when many of them became indifferent to all exertion. Day after day did the system of reduction continued, after the oldest and best experienced men in business considered it had reached its lowest possible limit. Some houses for a time gave up making goods at all, not so much for want of demand as from being literally ashamed to offer respectable workmen employment at a price at which they knew they could not exist; but it had no effect upon the cool speculators, who went on in their career, regardless of consequences, till all were drawn into the vortex. I sold goods that year, in a finished state, at 1s. per yard, which cost 4s. 6d. for *weaving only* in 1809. The effect of which was, to invert the order of reasoning of the theoretical economists, who assert that low prices invariably increase the quantity consumed. Those gentlemen forget that, in a highly excited and artificial (refined if they will) state of society, the demand for commodities is as much regulated by caprice, as necessity or usefulness, of which caprice our fair countrywomen have their share. In this instance the fact was fully verified; for, as soon as the price of articles, made chiefly for the consumption of the higher class of females, fell so very low, they would not purchase them at all, substituting others, of inferior utility, from France, at a much higher price and at any risk, which lessened the demand in all, and, in some instances, annihilated it altogether.

ving, had been refused support by the parishes, who would not recognise the principle of right*; that the consituted authorities and the upper classes were either utterly ignorant of the real condition of the people, or showed an apathy and indifference, to their wants, which was both unjustifiable and impolitic, as it had rendered them completely desperate and regardless of consequences. Mr. Finlay said, they knew that a considerable portion of distress existed; but it was not believed to be nearly to the extent which I described; that the reports, through the channels to which they had access, were so contradictory and unsatisfactory, that it was difficult to form any definite or correct opinion; that he was not friendly to the principle of parochial assessments, and subscriptions had been delayed as long as possible, for the purpose of not exciting false hopes, or abating exertion; but if things were really as bad as I described them, he wished me to see the sheriff of the county, and give him a statement of the facts, that he might be able to make an official report; and that the magitrates should immediately call a meeting and open a subscription for their relief. The sheriff afterwards waited upon me for the purpose, and a subscription was set on foot, which, in a few days, amounted to upwards of £.20,000; but it was now out of time; the people had assumed a menacing attitude, and attributed their conduct to

* This was the answer given to individuals, who, not being able to prosecute, they were obliged to associate themselves together, to try the law of the case, and endeavour to obtain, by collective, what was refused to individual, application. I was repeatedly consulted by many of the parties, and decidedly advised the measure as the only alternative left them, and my advice, in this matter, was afterwards made the ground of accusation against me, for being the general apostle of orginization, and mixed up with one of a very different character and complexion.

fear; whereas, if it had been done two or three months sooner, it would have been believed to have proceeded from commiseration for their sufferings.

The meeting of parliament was approaching, and exertions were making, in every part of the country, to have petitions, for reform, ready to be presented as early as possible after the opening of the session. It was in contemplation to request Mr. Finlay to present and support the prayer of the petition from Glasgow, and to this subject he turned the conversation. After some general remarks on the prevalence of opinions, in favour of reform, he, in a very imposing and emphatic manner, asked me to answer him, upon my honour, if I was not aware of the existence of an extensive and widely-spread secret conspiracy, for the avowed purpose of overturning the government. I solemnly assured him I was not; nor did I believe anything of the kind existed in Scotland; and, at all events, if it did, it was unconnected with the proceedings of the reform party, everything they intended being openly and publicly avowed; neither did I believe it possible a thing of that kind could go to any great extent, without coming to my knowledge; for, from the nature of my connexions, (although I might not be solicited to become a member of such an association,) I was convinced that, from one quarter or another, I should have heard of it, or been consulted, as to its practicability. He then assured me, that government had the most positive and undoubted information of the existence of such a conspiracy, although they did not then know all the particulars, but were certain that many thousands, in Glasgow and its neighbourhood, were engaged in it; that he believed there might be many things wrong in our system of government, but there was no possibility of amending them by such means; that, relying on my *good sense* and general knowledge of the population, he had made the communication to me, it being in my power to render a most important service to society, and a duty incumbent upon me, to use my influence and make every exertion to suppress it. I observed, I was still sceptical as to its existence, and, at all events, was not such a sciolist as to believe it had gone to the extent he had represented; that I was equally convinced, with him, of the absurdity and utter hopelessness of doing any good by such means; that I considered nothing could better serve the purpose of the ministry, and those opposed to every species of reform, than such an attempt; as it would serve as a pretext for throwing discredit on its advocates; and quashing the demand then so generally made; which, from its universality, if moderately and temperately conducted, afforded hopes of succeeding to some rational and practicable extent; that, for the purpose of disappointing them, but more especially to prevent those who were starving from becoming the victims of such delusion, I would do everything in my power; adding, if it existed at all, it must be confined to that class of society whose situation I had described; that I might not be able to learn particulars, but felt confident that I could soon ascertain the general fact, and pledged myself to let him know the result of my enquiries, whether they were confirmatory or contradictory to the information they had received.

The reform committees were now keeping up an active correspondence, but I was certain that nothing of a secret nature was mixed up with their proceedings. In the city of Glasgow, the parties engaged in the active management were men in business, and the greater portion of them repectable in their situations in life: with all of them I was personally acquainted; knew every proceeding, and their general knowledge and information I considered a sufficient guarantee that they would not (even individually) embark in any desperate measure. The various suburbs were petitioning separately; but, as their committees were composed of the more intelligent class of workmen, I entertained no suspicion of them. The management of the applications for parochial aid had fallen into the hands of some furious profligate fanatics, with just a sufficient portion of ability to give them an influence over the very lowest class, who, from positive sufferings, believed they could save themselves from drowning, by grasping at a straw. They had been holding tumultuous meetings in the suburbs, and it immediately occurred to me, that, if anything foolish or imprudent was going on, it was amongst them; and to that quarter I directed my enquiries, and soon found my conjectures confirmed. I was personally known by the greater portion of the labouring population, and was fully aware of the impropriety of appearing publicly amongst them. I therefore determined to confine my enquiries to a single individual, who, I had reason to suspect, was acquainted with the real measures contemplated, and depended upon my own address for getting to the bottom of them. The man I selected for this purpose was an operative weaver, of the name of M'Lachlan, who was not previously known to me. He was in extreme poverty, and had been taking a lead at the meetings held for enforcing their claims upon the parishes. With very little difficulty, I soon learned his view of the matter: he informed me, that the people had been tantalised with hopes of relief, until they were reduced to despair; that they were now convinced everything depended upon themselves, and they were determined to take measures to redress their own wrongs; that a secret organization had been some time before entered into, for that purpose; and that the public meetings were held, to give them an opportunity of operating upon the minds of the people, and, under that cover, to enable them to make proselytes. He boasted of the extent of their numbers and resources, and directly threatened, that, if those men (myself included) who were capable of influencing the people would not come forward and direct their measures, they would not long have an opportunity, it being determined not to allow them to do so afterwards, and to punish such as remained neutral. I could not, at that time, press my enquiries to obtain a knowledge of particulars, but told him, the people ought to beware of committing any violence, which would only bring destruction upon their own heads, and cautioned him against letting any of his colleagues know that he had made such a communication to me. I did not give credit to everything this man told me, but I could not allow myself to doubt the general fact, that an organization was in progress. I believed that, on the part of government, a greater alarm had been excited than there was any just ground for; while, on the other hand, it was evident that a part of the policy of the other party was to exaggerate the amount of their numbers and means, for the purpose of gaining an accession of strength. I knew, however, the materials were inflammable, and only required ignition to produce an explosion; it was, therefore, the impression upon my mind, that no time was to be lost in taking measures to prevent the conflagration from bursting. Agreeable to promise, I communicated what I had learnt to Mr. Finlay, without letting him know the source from which I derived my information, farther than from what class of society any danger was to be apprehended, and advised that every exertion should be made to relieve their distress, as the best means of lessening the influence of those who were attempting to mislead them. Mr. Finlay again urged it upon me, as a duty, to lend my assistance, in preserving the public peace; when I told him, as I did not believe there was any immediate danger, before condescending upon any detailed measures of prevention, it was necessary to ascertain the actual progress of the organization, which I recommended should be done without delay, when I would render any advice my knowledge of the country and population enabled me. On the 18th of December I went to New Lanark, where I remained until the 22d. During the time I continued with Mr. Owen, we went over the whole practical and theoretical details of his system. The visit gave mutual satisfaction, and it was agreed that I should take the charge of conducting the new arrangements he contemplated, the amount of salary alone being left undetermined*. Mr. Finlay had requested me not to close finally with Mr. Owen during my visit, and wished to see me immediately on my return. I called upon him the same evening, and, after disposing of the subject of my visit to Mr. Owen, he recurred to public affairs. He said, they had made no progress in gaining information during my absence, and the consternation and alarm were daily increasing among the higher classes, in consequence of the threats held out and the menacing appearance the people had assumed; that it was impossible to impose any check, with-

* It may be proper to mention here, that, during this visit, while conversing on the general state of the country, I informed Mr. Owen what Mr. Finlay had requested me to do, and what I had learned was going forward, and, on my return, I acquainted Mr. Finlay I had done so.

out ascertaining who were the leaders; and he considered my personal assistance was essential to enable them to do so. I answered, that, however necessary he might consider my assistance, it was a matter which might involve too serious consequences, for me to engage in, without consulting my friends, and I therefore wished to refer to Mr. Cockburn and Mr. Jeffrey, for their opinions. To this proposition he, however, strongly objected: he said that, confiding in my honour, he had intrusted me with an important state secret, believing it was in my power to render a very important service to the country; and, although the gentlemen mentioned were honourable, upright men, and might make no improper use of the information, their political opinions differed from those who had the government of the country in their hands, and it would therefore be highly improper to let them know anything of the matter. He then added, that he had now the authority of government, to offer me *a respectable, permanent situation,* if I would lend my assistance to suppress the conspiracy. I told him, if he had not known enough of me before, to prevent him from making such a proposition, the respect he owed to the gentleman, whose letter had introduced me to him, on that occasion, ought to have protected me from insult; that he already knew I was incapable of acting from such a motive; and that the only one which could induce me to interfere at all, would be to endeavour to save a set of men who, goaded on by their necessities, were rashly and ignorantly exposing themselves to punishment; that, in the event of doing so, the only reward I wished was, the approbation of good and upright men, upon whom I could call, if ever I was placed in such a situation, in after life, as to require their assistance.

I continued, that I felt very confident I was able to dissipate the conspiracy, without the necessity of inflicting punishment on any one, and without its existence ever being publicly known; that, to an absolute certainty, I could effectually prevent the possibility of any explosion; but that my farther interference depended upon certain stipulations being complied with, and a rigid adherence to the plans I should propose. The first of these was, that, if I failed in inducing the people to abandon their foolish project, and it became necessary to take any of them into custody, all those with whom I came in contact, or who might be either directly or indirectly, influenced by my proceedings, or those who might be employed, should be secure from punishment, however guilty they had been previously. Second, that I should have full liberty to try the extent of my influence, without any premature interference on their part, unless there was an actual danger of open disturbance, and when I could no longer be responsible for the public peace. Third, that in no case was I to appear in any prosecution, or be called upon to give evidence. And fourth, that, whichever way the matter terminated, Messrs. Jeffrey and Cockburn should be made acquainted with the whole of my proceedings. These stipulations being most solemnly agreed to, I proposed, that they should find a few men, to become members of the confederacy, and, for the purpose of preventing any deception or collusion, that none of them should know of another being employed; by which means the information given by one would be checked by another. In this way I calculated, that timely notice could be received before any real danger approached, and, at the same time, find out the quarters where my influence could be most promptly and effectually exerted, to induce them to abandon their scheme. That I should have no communication with the persons so employed, neither should they know anything of me, and as everything depended upon profound secresy, I would hold no intercourse with any person filling an official situation under government. All these points were approved and agreed upon, and Mr. Reddie was substituted for the sheriff of the county, to whom and Mr. Finlay all my intercourse was confined. As a check upon the whole, the line of conduct I marked out for myself was, to get into the confidence of one person, who had influence amongst them, and was acquainted with the arcana of the business, which, as soon as I had effected, I should be able to convince of its absurdity, and make him instrumental in persuading the others to abandon it; for which purpose I determined to ply M'Lachlan, who had already committed himself to me. In effecting this object, two difficulties presented themselves. I could not obtain his confidence in any other manner, than by allowing him to believe I approved of the measures they were pursuing, and, if I did so, it would naturally occur that I ought to come forward, with all my influence, in their support; but this objection I obviated, by saying, I was too well known to make any prominent appearance. Next, that, although I might secure him personally from danger, he might be the means of instigating others, and extending the conspiracy by the indirect encouragement he received from me, before I had him sufficiently in my power; but this apparent difficulty I made the chief means of preventing the extension of the organization. My proceedings required to be conducted with the utmost caution. Being aware of the man's situation, (although not yet sufficiently acquainted with his personal character,) I gave him small sums of money, to relieve his necessities, regulated so as not to excite suspicion, as being above what I was able to afford. So far this had the effect, but I soon found him so completely worthless, that I could attach little credit to any of his statements. My first object was, to ascertain how far the organization extended through the country; if there were any persons of repectability or intelligence connected with it; if any correspondence had taken place with the manufacturing counties of England, then also in a state of ferment; and to adapt my measures to the circumstances. However, after having several conferences with this man, I found his statements so incredible and incongruous, so much at variance, at one time compared with another, that I was unable to arrive at any thing definite, and, after losing nearly a fortnight, contrary to my original intention, I was obliged to make him introduce me to another of the party.

I was also completely deceived in the opinion I had formed, when the government could not furnish a single individual capable of getting admission amongst them, although I had pointed out the quarters which I thought accessible; for, like many others, I imagined they had always at hand a number of experienced agents, to meet any exigency. By many persons it may be considered creditable to our government, that they were not so provided; but of this I must be allowed to express my doubt. With those who consider the prevention of crime preferable to its punishment, some such means of doing it will always be considered necessary, and, until society is differently constituted, and governments have recourse to the primary principle of ameliorating the condition of the people, and resting the means of prevention in a superior education, and the diffusion of a better system of practical morality, I see no other remedy. Judging from the particular case before us, two or three intelligent persons, that could have been fully depended upon, would have been of more benefit than a whole host of such men as they employed, and would have avoided the positive evil they committed. They produced all the bad effects that can result from an organized system of espionage, (which, in any shape or degree, is an evil only to be tolerated in the most extreme cases of necessity,) without any of the good. The gang, let loose upon this occasion, belonged chiefly to the police establishment of Edinburgh, the local officers being too well known. They were not made acquainted with particulars, but were given to understand there were some secret measures going on against the government, which they were to endeavour, by all means, to discover; the local officers also got a general notification, which, without being of any service, enabled them to assist in the howl, and add to the mass of misrepresentation. Such men might be qualified to associate with and ferret out thieves, but could form no conception of and were unfit to be intrusted with an affair of national importance; they frequented taprooms and public-houses, overheard the conversation of isolated individuals, with their passions excited and irritated by suffering. Immediately a report was made, that *a great number* of persons were assembled in such a house plotting to overturn the government; one heard there were secret meetings here; another there were arms concealed there; a third, that there was to be a general insurrection on such a day, or such a night, until the magistrates were put into such a state of terror and alarm, that it was with difficulty they could be convinced I could give them notice, in time, to prevent them from being assassinated *. These vague rumours and alarms brought informations from a thousand quarters. I had scarcely a friend or acquaintance, whose political opinions were known to be liberal, that was not denounced, and whose real character I had not to explain and defend. It was not the least curious part of this solemn farce, that my own proceedings were traced and reported upon, and I was frequently treated, on an evening, with a portrait of my character, that rendered it difficult for me to discover my own identity. Yet, upon no better authority, representations of the state of the provinces are frequently made, forwarded to the Secretary of State, put into a green bag, and gravely submitted to the Committees of Parliament, who legislate upon them, never for a moment doubting the possibility of the inaccuracy of a report made by the resident magistracy, unmindful of the axiom applied to philosophers by the ingenious author of Lacon, that magistrates, like travellers, are often better informed, as to what is going on abroad than at home.

The name of the second person, to whom I found it necessary to be introduced, was Campbell; and, as he subsequently made a conspicuous

* The magistrates of Glasgow were not in the secret, depending wholly upon Messrs. Finlay and Reddie, who assured them they were in correspondence with a person who would apprise them when any serious danger approached. This assurance, however, was not always sufficient to allay their apprehension. The Lord Provost was so much alarmed, that he would not sleep in his own house for several nights, although assured, by his friends, he was in perfect safety. On one occasion I was waited for, at eleven o'clock at night; as he would not venture to his bed, until Mr. Finlay actually saw the person, in consequence of some rumours he had heard during the day. These rumours were purposely set afloat, to deceive the magistrates, and even Mr. Finlay, although apprised it was a part of the policy, was not always free from their influence, daily references being made to me to ascertain the truth.

figure in the Court of Justiciary, and his conduct became the subject of a motion in Parliament, I will describe his situation and character, as far as they came under my observation. He was also an operative weaver, in extreme poverty, but had previously been more favourably situated; naturally shrewd and firm in character, his information and judgment were above mediocrity; tinctured with enthusiasm, the difficulties of his situation had blinded his judgment, and he felt confident of success in the scheme they were pursuing. I found him cautious, and, for a time, ambiguous; but, in comparing all his statements, never found him violate truth. I had no previous knowledge of him, but soon discovered he was much better adapted to my purpose than M'Lachlan, and I took the same method of getting into his confidence, by occasionally giving him small sums of money. I never entertained a doubt, from the good sense he possessed, of being able to convince him of the absurdity of the measures they were pursuing: it however required both time and caution, as I should have lost all influence over him, had he at first entertained the least suspicion of my real design. Much has been said of my instigating these men, in the preliminary part of my proceedings; but such was not the fact. They certainly, for a time, believed me friendly to the measure. Any directions, however, which I gave them (although they were unconscious of it,) were a direct check upon the organization, which would have extended with greater rapidity, had it been left to its natural course. M'Lachlan had represented to me, that their connexion extended over all the western counties of Scotland, and through part of Stirling, Perth and Forfar shires; that they were in correspondence with the manufacturing counties of England, they being similarly organized; that many people, of property and respectability, were connected with them; and that they had a considerable quantity of arms provided. This was a delusion which the leaders practised upon the members of the confederacy, as well as every person they solicited to join them; when, in point of fact, it never extended beyond the neighbourhood of Glasgow. It required a considerable time to correct those misrepresentations, which I accomplished partly by Campbell, as I progressively got into his confidence, and partly by other means. I was, however, obliged to obtain this information indirectly, and by piecemeal; for, when I asked a direct question, I was pressed to become a member, and they would acquaint me with everything. In these cases, I had to repeat my reasons for declining, and gave them the strongest injunctions not to let any of their associates know that I had any knowledge of their proceedings. From my acquaintance with the leading men in the manufacturing towns and villages, in Scotland and several parts of England, they constantly solicited me to point out the proper persons for them to apply to, who were most likely to be useful in extending the organization. To keep up appearances, I several times complied with their request, and, in some instances, advised such delegations, but gave the names of men who, I knew, had too much judgment and prudence to engage in it; and where I had any fear of their coming in contact with persons who might be misled by their misrepresentations, I previously gave those persons warning, and put them upon their guard*; so

* As this will probably meet the eye of a person who was, at the time, secretary to the Reform Committee of a certain town, of some note, and a correspondent of Major Cartwright, I would remind him that he ought to have had the candour to acknowledge

that, in no instance, did they succeed, which tantalized and disgusted the parties sent upon missions, fomented divisions, and exhausted the trifling funds they were able to command. I did not condescend to use dissimulation, by any arguments in favour of their plans. I obtained all my information by pointing out difficulties, and bringing forward objections. I knew the whole history of the organization formed in Ireland, which led to the rebellion in 1798, and the attempt in 1803, as well as those formed in England and Scotland, from 1793 to 1798, both from the public documents, and from personal acquaintance with parties who had been actors in them all. I produced the minutes of evidence taken by the Parliamentary Committees, to show them the impossibility of any secret organization existing without coming to the knowledge of government, which had the effect of shaking their faith, and making them condescend more particularly on the means they had taken to avoid detection; but, like all other persons, similarly situated, they believed they were a great deal wiser than those who had gone before them.

After being introduced to Campbell, I paid little more attention to M'Lachlan, than merely to keep him in countenance, and finding the total inefficiency of the whole tribe of emissaries employed by *authority,* I was obliged to point out a person who I thought competent to the purpose, and the channel through which I believed he might be induced to engage in the undertaking. This person was personally known to me, but had

the caution I gave him, in place of assisting, in the hue and cry that was raised against me, for being an instigator. I am not ignorant of the perverted statements and misrepresentations sent to Mr. Wooler and the editors of several other papers, as well as different members of parliament, nor of the reason why they had not all the effect that was desired by the writers.

no knowledge of my having pointed him out for the employment; nor had I any communication whatever with him relative to it, his reports being made to Mr. Finlay and Mr. Reddie, and by them communicated to me. He was employed early in January, 1817; it was, however, about the end of that month, or the beginning of February, before he was admitted a member, from which period their meetings were regularly attended, and collateral information being received from other quarters, by the middle of February the true state of the matter came to be accurately known. By that time I had succeeded so completely with Campbell, that he had thrown off all reserve, so that the checks to all attempts at misrepresentation, by any single party, were so multiplied, that deception could no longer be practised. From the moment I got fully into his confidence, I turned round upon him, using every argument I was master of, to show him the utter impossibility of reforming the government by the means they were pursuing, and the positive certainty of such pursuits ending in their own ruin and destruction. I used similar arguments to M'Lachlan; but not considering him of much consequence, I did not take the same pains to convince him. With Campbell I had completely succeeded: he had not only agreed to give it up himself, but had engaged to use his influence with the others to do so also. Events, however, occurred in another quarter, which baffled all my calculations.

Being satisfied in my own mind, that I would come to a final agreement with Mr. Owen, I commenced winding up my private business immediately, on my return from Lanark, in December, as formerly mentioned. Mr. Finlay considered it would be proper to have a specific salary agreed upon, sufficient to command the necessary degree of comfort and respectability; and his view being, to leave nothing in a state of uncertainty, he wrote to Mr. Owen, early in January, stating his opinion of the amount he considered me entitled to. Mr. Owen immediately wrote me, in return, that he conceived we were perfectly competent to settle our own business, without the interference of a third party; and, after the interchange of several letters, it was arranged to meet, in Mr. Finlay's house, on the 19th of January, for the purpose of closing the engagement. When we met, on that occasion, Mr. Owen said, that salary was a matter of such minor consideration, that it never ought to be named; that the improvements he contemplated were too important, to render that an object; and, as he felt perfectly satisfied with me, if I chose to leave the arrangements to him, he would secure to me all the comfort and respectability which a situation of so much importance required. I had previously consulted Mr. Jeffrey, Mr. Cockburn and my other friends, and, as they fully approved of my closing the engagement, I, without hesitation, agreed; making no other stipulation than, in case of any accident occurring to him, I should be secured in six months' salary corresponding with the rate my expenses were found to require. Mr. Owen was in a short time going to London, to propose those plans to parliament and the public, which have since excited so much interest; and, as we had fully concocted everything respecting them, he wished me to complete my arrangements with as much celerity as possible, that I might be able to take my charge before he went away. Early in February, I succeeded in getting my private business arranged in such a manner, that a visit or two to Glasgow would have enabled me to finish it. I calculated also that, from my situation at

Lanark, I could have prosecuted my plan for the dissolution of the confederacy, with equal advantage as if I had remained in Glasgow. It never was my intention to appear personally amongst the party, or attend their meetings, unless all other means of inducing them to dissolve it had failed. My view was, to do everything by the agency of others, and, as I then knew nearly its extent and the description of people engaged, I considered I could bring my influence to bear, with equal force and less suspicion. I could not, however, get Mr. Finlay and Mr. Reddie convinced of the propriety of my leaving Glasgow. They said they could not conduct matters properly without my assistance, and had no confidence, unless I remained upon the spot; and, after a good deal of argument, I at length complied with their request; and, acquainting Mr. Owen with the delay, very reluctantly allowed him to proceed to London without my removing.

It will now be proper to narrate, more particularly, the origin and progress of the confederacy. From all the information obtained, it appeared to have commenced immediately after the meeting held at Thrush Grove, in the neighbourhood of Glasgow, on the 29th October, 1816, which has already been described. A very strong excitement was produced by that event, and some persons, in Calton, (one of the suburbs of Glasgow, who were in desperate circumstances,) entertaining an idea that parliament would pay no attention to the petitions for reform and redress of grievances, unless means were taken to compel them, entered into a mutual agreement to adopt more efficient measures, to force a reform, which they believed was not to be obtained in any other manner. It was never precisely ascertained what number there were at the commencement, their own accounts varying considerably; for, while they believed they were likely to succeed, all were anxious to assume the merit of being one of the original founders. They had no specific plan, or well defined object, in view; but they bound themselves, under a secret obligation, not to divulge any proposition, made by any of the members. They were deeply impressed with the belief, that a government that had placed them in such a situation, must have been weakly and partially administered; which view they considered so just and reasonable in itself, that it could never be doubted by others; that there was, therefore, nothing to oppose a change but a very few persons, directly supported by the system of corruption, who were comparatively so trifling in number, and so contemptible in themselves, that they could offer no effectual resistance; that it was only necessary for the suffering classes, to understand one another, to enable them to drive the corruptionists from the helm, and take upon themselves the government, which they were much better qualified to reform and administer. However ridiculous and absurd these opinions may appear, it is not the less true, that they existed. None but minute and accurate observers are aware of the peculiarity of character and opinions, produced by insulated association among the different ranks of men, and their absolute ignorance respecting the true character and feelings of each other, as society is at present constituted. These men saw nothing but misery and distress among the great mass of the people around them; the public press informed them, that all the country was in a similar situation; and that this distress and unequal distribution had their origin in the errors of our institutions, and the mal-administration of our government. Under such circumstances, what conclusion could they draw; but that it was only the few, interested in the continuance of the system, who did not desire a change, against whom, they considered, was ranged the interest of the whole labouring population and physical power of the country. Hearing only one opinion, it was not to be supposed they could calculate the difficulty of bringing this force to bear, admitting it to have been united in sentiment; and an enlightened government, on viewing the total inadequacy of their means to effect their purpose, might have found it necessary to keep them under restraint, but it would have considered them fitter subjects for a lunatic asylum than a scaffold. Amongst them were some men, who had been members of the unions in Ireland and Scotland, at the periods formerly alluded to, and something upon a similar principle to the affiliated societies of that time naturally suggested itself; but, although the plan they adopted was nearly the same, it attained nothing like the extent or perfection of organization of those associations. Neither the absolute amount of their numbers, nor its progressive advance, was accurately known, even by themselves; for, in this, as well as in many other things, they deceived each other. They had, at first, all assembled together, and, as their numbers increased, they formed small primary societies, consisting of from twelve to sixteen members. A delegate from a certain number of the primary societies formed a divisional committee, who again sent one delegate, to form a central or general committee. For the executive, or general government, the central committee appointed a select one, by ballot, whose names were only known to the secretary and treasurer; but the whole organization was more nominal than real, they having neither ability nor means to render it efficient. It was a part of the plan, that small sums, such as a penny per week, should be collected from each member; but the general poverty prevented them from carrying it into execution; and they never had, at any one time, ten shillings in the hands of the treasurer. An obligation, to keep all the proceedings secret, was taken by every member, on admission. Signs and words were agreed upon, to enable them to distinguish each other; and, according to their own account, these forms were more than once changed and modified. As the ulterior proceedings, in parliament and before the Court of Justiciary, depended more upon the form than upon the substance, I shall distinctly state how the information was obtained. When the person, whom I caused to be employed, was admitted a member, it was found, that an obligation was first exacted, not to disclose what should be afterwards revealed; and then the oath, or bond of union, explaining the nature and purpose of the association, was administered. This corresponded with the general account given me by Campbell; but, to prevent deception, it was necessary to get a confirmation from more points than one. I had never condescended upon the particulars, but, as he had, by this time, communicated all the general facts to me and put himself completely in my power, I took the first opportunity of ascertaining the details, which agreed exactly with the other account*. These statements being only verbal, Mr.

* Let me here remark, that I have no intention to blink the question, by having recourse to any jesuitical casuistry or metaphysical subtility, to justify myself by the evasion of any matter of form. I despise all such canting hyprocritical artifice. I consider the implied confidence placed in me in exactly the same light as if a thousand forms had been gone through, and if a higher and purer motive cannot be assigned for my moral justification, and if the proofs of that motive cannot be collected, from this detail of cir-

Finlay expressed great anxiety to obtain a copy, from some of the members, in writing; and, a short time after, the person alluded to procured one for him from one of the parties. I never saw either this, or any other copy, in writing. It was, however, the identical document that made such a noise in the House of Commons, and was, I believe, perfectly correct. It made a very imposing appearance at the time; but as it has, like many other things that have served their purpose, long been consigned to the tomb of all the Capulets, I will here transcribe it, for the purpose of refreshing the memory of my readers.

"In the awful presence of God, I, A. B., do voluntarily swear, that I will persevere in my endeavouring to form a brotherhood of affection, amongst Britons of every description, who are considered worthy of confidence; and that I will persevere in my endeavours to obtain, for all the people in Great Britain and Ireland, not disqualified by crimes or insanity, the elective franchise at the age of twenty-one, with free and equal representation, and annual parliaments; and that I will support the same to the utmost of my power, either by moral or physical strength, as the case may require. And I do farther swear, that neither hopes, fears, rewards nor punishments shall induce me to inform on, or give evidence against, any member or members, collectively or individually, for any act or expression done or made, in or out, in this or similar societies, under the punishment of death, to be inflicted on me by any

cumstances, I leave myself open to the unconditional reprobation of those whose system of ethics is founded upon the trick and juggle of evasion, the essence of whose religion is hypocrisy, and the virtue of whose characters consists in the ingenuity and dexterity of concealment.

member or members of such societies. So help me God, and keep me steadfast."

Formidable and awful as this obligation may appear, upon paper, as the matter developed itself, it was found to exist more in name than in reality. During the whole of the month of January, and a few days in February, while the extent of the confederacy was but imperfectly known, by assembling occasionally all those who were unemployed in the suburbs of Glasgow, under the pretext of promoting the prosecutions against the parishes, they had succeeded in keeping up anxiety and alarm; but, upon getting to the bottom of all their pretexts and deceptions, I found that no person, of respectability or influence, even among the labouring classes, was connected with them. That a very few of the better informed, of that description, had been deceived, by their misrepresentations, to become members; but, as soon as they learnt the real state of the fact, they immediately withdrew; and, with the exception of a very few persons, in some of the surrounding villages, it had extended to no other part of the country.

All the towns, petitioning for reform, had appointed standing committees, and were keeping up an active correspondence with one another; but they had no connexion whatever with this confederacy. From the appearance of the metropolis and some of the northern counties, I had all along felt great anxiety to know the true state of their relations with England, feeling conscious it would not be so easy to induce them to break up the organization, if operated upon by any external influence. Every means were taken to evade this point with me, by ambiguous expressions and inuendoes, until they could no longer conceal the true state of the case, when they admitted, they had no intercourse with England whatever, and had only made use of it, as a stratagem, to induce people to join them*. They were anxious to conceal this, as long as possible, in the hope they would be able to raise money to dispatch delegates to England. I latterly encouraged the idea of this delegation; for, had it been necessary, I calculated upon thereby cutting off their last hope. They knew nothing of the country, nor the persons to apply to, and whoever they might have sent upon the mission, I could have had entirely at my disposal. From the first week in February, their meetings were attended, and regular reports made of their proceedings, and having, by that means, obtained a complete command over them, by the 13th or 14th, I was fully acquainted with every particular.

As my knowledge of the actual circumstances increased, the difficulties diminished, and, having now learnt the extent of the field I had to act upon, I considered the proper time had arrived, to take direct measures to suppress it. On the 16th I had a long conference with Campbell, when I abandoned all indirect arguments. I placed before him, in the strongest point of view, the utter hopelessness and impracticability of suc-

* Mystery has a much more powerful influence over the human mind than reality, and has always been more successfully practised. The deceptions which the French emigrants practised upon each other at Coblentz, (as related by Las Cases,) was acted, over again, in this instance. A report was circulated, that they were to get possession of a depôt of arms, amounting to 15,000 stand, which had been provided by the organization of 1793, and had remained concealed, in good condition, from that time; and, ridiculous as it may appear, it was believed by many. The exposure of one deception does not prevent the success of another; for, the same delusions, which were practised at this period, were successful again, in 1819 and 1820. A government, however, is unjustifiable, that either makes it a pretext, or allows itself to be duped and precipitated into obnoxious measures, by such absurd reports or false alarms.

ceeding in their scheme, and the positive evil that would result, to society and themselves, if they persisted. I succeeded in convincing him of the impropriety of farther personal interference, and my next step was, to induce him to use what influence he possessed, to make his associates act in a similar manner. I had learned, that he and M'Lachlan had been parties to it from its first commencement, and that they were members of the *nominal* central committee; that the confederacy had been kept alive by the exertions of a very few persons, with all of whom he was personally acquainted; and he felt confident, his leaving them would have considerable influence; that, as they had been completely deceived, in not getting any persons, of property or ability, to join them in Scotland, all their hopes now rested on opening a communication with England, where they expected to meet with more encouragement; for which purpose, they were in treaty with one or two persons, in superior circumstances, who had held out hopes of advancing as much money as to enable them to defray the expense of a delegation to Carlisle. This rendered my calculation certain. I then felt secure, even if they should succeed in raising the necessary sum, it would afford me the means of defeating them effectually.

For the purpose of strengthening Campbell's determination, I saw him upon the 19th, and again on the 21st, and completely confirmed him in his resolution. Through the medium of the person attending their meetings, I was apprised the central committee was to meet on the evening of the 22d. This information was confirmed to me by Campbell, when he faithfully promised it would be the last meeting he should attend; and he was to embrace the opportunity it afforded, of reasoning with those of his associates whom he considered of most consequence, to endeavour to detach them also from the confederacy. I never saw this person afterwards, and I will now relate the proceedings, which occurred in another quarter, during this last eventful week.

I was in the practice of meeting Mr. Finlay and Mr. Reddie, every second or third evening, or oftener, as the case might require. These meetings took place, first, in Mr. Finlay's house, and afterwards, to avoid suspicion, in that of Mr. Reddie, where the various reports they received were discussed, and misrepresentations corrected. On the evenings of the 17th and 19th of February, I informed them of the progress I had made with Campbell, and the confident hope I entertained, of being able to dissipate the confederacy, in a very short time, without the necessity of having recourse to coercive measures. I also pointed out the advantages that might be derived from the delegation to England, admitting them to be able to carry it into effect. On the evening of the 21st, I repeated this assurance, in a still stronger manner, my confidence daily increasing with the knowledge of every new fact. The Report of the Secret Committee of the House of Lords had, that day, arrived in Glasgow, and Mr. Reddie presented it, for my perusal, requesting my opinion as to the effect it was likely to produce. I told him, I believed it would make a very strong impression; for, although it did not mention Glasgow in the list of disaffected places, it would be seen that government was in possession of specific information as to the situation of the places named in England; and I was therefore of opinion, it would act as a powerful auxiliary, in deterring persons from assisting, or joining the confederacy. My opinion seemed to give perfect satisfaction; and, in consequence of having a full knowledge of every transaction, and no danger being to be apprehended, it was agreed I should proceed with my plan, to break it up as soon as possible. I was to meet them again on the evening of the 23d; but the reader may judge of my astonishment and surprise, when the report reached me, on the morning of that day, that the whole of the parties were taken into custody, at the meeting, the previous evening, and were then lodged in jail.

Judging this proceeding apart from any breach of faith with me, it was either intended, or it was taken advantage of, to make it form a very prominent feature in the general measures of the period; and, as various opinions may be formed of the merits, or demerits, of the parties concerned, to enable a more correct conclusion to be drawn, I will give a brief summary of other events which appear to have been connected with it.

I have already frequently alluded to the general ferment in the country, and the efforts made by the advocates for reform to have petitions ready by the meeting of parliament. On the 20th of January, Cashman was found guilty of felony, at the Old Bailey Sessions, arising out of the riots at the Spafield meeting on the 2d of December. At the same time a charge of conspiracy was preferred against Dr. Watson and some others, who traversed. On the 22d, a meeting of delegates, from various quarters of the country, was held in London, for the purpose of coming to a definite arrangement on the heads of a reform bill, to be brought into parliament, which was to meet on the 28th. In the speech from the throne, no mention was made of disaffection, but the Prince Regent, in returning from the House of Lords, was attacked and insulted by the rabble; and on the 3d of February, a message was sent to both houses of parliament, describing many parts of the country as being in a disturbed state, and secret committees were moved for, to receive the necessary information and report. Within a few days after the meeting of parliament, above one thousand petitions, for reform and retrenchment, were presented, signed by more than half a million of persons. On the 6th, the secret committees were appointed, and on the 7th, Watson, Preston, *Castles*, &c. were apprehended, by warrant of the Secretary of State. On the 10th, the third Spafield meeting was held, where Mr. Hunt vilified all the leading reformers. On the 14th, Castles was said to have made *disclosures*, and Watson, Preston, &c. were committed to the Tower, under a charge of high treason. At the same time, a reward of 500*l.* each was offered for the apprehension of Thistlewood and young Watson, upon a similar charge. On the 18th, the Lords' Committee made their report, which stated, that secret societies existed at Manchester, Nottingham, Sheffield, Leicester, &c., who were in communication with others of the same description in London. On the 19th, the Committee of the House of Commons made a more detailed report. It stated, there was a general plan of insurrection by the organized societies, which extended over all the northern counties of England; that arms were provided to a considerable extent in London; *that at Glasgow, and several other towns in Scotland, secret societies also existed, where they made use of the reform meetings, as a cover for their real design; that they were in correspondence with England, and were to act simultaneously with it; and they had likewise arms provided.* On the 21st, a Bill, to suspend the Habeas Corpus Act, was notified in the House of Lords, which was passed on the 24th. On the 26th, the account of the arrests in Glasgow arrived in London, and the same evening the first reading of the Suspension Bill came on in the House of Commons. It had been agreed, in the Secret Committee, that the oath or obligation of the confederacy at Glasgow should not be made public; but the ministry being pressed in the debate to show more substantial proofs of the disaffection which they asserted existed in the country, the Lord Advocate of Scotland rose in his place, and, with the greatest solemnity, *read the document formerly transcribed,* which produced a strong sensation in the house. This was a proof positive, that could not be resisted, particularly when he added, *that there were many of the higher orders of society engaged in the conspiracy, and that it consisted of many thousands!* The unbelieving members were silenced and were afraid to show a scepticism, which might call forth something still more horrifying, and on the 28th the bill passed the house *without farther enquiry!*

On the morning of the 23d of February, the account of the apprehension of the parties at the meeting came upon me like a thunderbolt. All the consequences rushed upon my mind with the withering influence of the Sirocco. I saw all my plans, to convince these deluded men of the absurdity of their conduct, and my attempt to save them from punishment, frustrated, when success had become almost certain, and myself relentlessly and unfeelingly compromised and sacrificed. I was at once fully aware of the intention of the measure, and it was obvious to me, if the case could be established for the ministry, little regard would be paid to the manner it would operate upon me, and from the narrow circle to which I had confined the information, and the manner I had reason to believe it had been communicated, I calculated to a certainty on being exposed. After the breach of faith with me, I should have been justified in making a public exposure of the whole, but it would have been of no benefit to myself, and done a positive injury to the parties accused. In the heat and irritation of the public mind, my motives would have been misconstrued and perverted by all parties, and I should have got credit from none. Those who were friendly to a reform in the representation (among whom almost all my personal friends were numbered), would have considered any connexion whatever with the party opposed, however much good it might have accomplished, or however pure my motives, of itself sufficient to damn me. If the disclosure was calculated to militate against the measures of the ministry, all their partizans would have turned round upon me, endeavoured to invalidate my testimony, and held me up as a person unworthy of credit; while a statement of the facts would have been no justification, and would have seriously prejudiced the case of the accused before trial, even admitting I had acted as an *instigator* or *participator* in the crime charged. In that view, I determined to remain silent, however much I might suffer; to exert all my influence, which I considered would rather be increased than diminished by the fear of exposing their conduct, to check all false information; and, above all, to prevent any prosecution being instituted against those with whom I had communicated, or who had been directly or indirectly influenced, by the conduct of any persons employed.

In these cogitations, almost bursting with indignation, I passed that, to me, memorable and miserable day, waiting with impatience for the time of appointment, to hear what justification Mr. Finlay could make for his conduct. When the hour at last arrived, I hastened to the house of Mr. Reddie, where I met Mr. Finlay. Irritated almost to fury, I branded him with a breach of the agreement, made with me, in taking the men into custody, when in the full knowledge of everything being perfectly safe, and for uselessly and unnecessarily compromising me. He first endeavoured to pacify me, and then to justify himself, he said, that peremptory instructions had been received, from Lord Sidmouth, to apprehend all the parties immediately, on the receipt of the order. I replied, that was no reason why confidence should have been broken with me, and that I had a right to have been consulted before they proceeded to put it in execution. He said their reason for not doing so was, *that they were aware I would not give my consent, and as they were obliged to act, they thought it better to do it without my knowledge.* Another reason assigned was, that the report of the Secret Committee of the House of Commons would show the conspirators that government was acquainted with their proceedings, which might deter them from meeting again, *so that they would not have had another opportunity of finding them together!* I said, if it had produced that effect, it was all that was required, and would have answered the purpose much better than the manner in which they had acted; but my reasoning could not recal the past, nor alter the general measures, of which this was only a part. I determined, however, to render the number of sufferers as small as possible, and to do all in my power to mitigate punishment which I could not altogether avert.

On learning the particulars, I found that seventeen or eighteen persons had been apprehended at the meeting, and several more at their own houses, during the night. A list of their names was shown to me, but, with the exception of Campbell and M'Lachlan, I had no personal knowledge of any other, and I insisted that they should be set at liberty, agreeable to the pledge given me. Mr. Finlay said that, as they were as guilty as any of the others, long before I had ever seen them, he thought I ought not to insist in protecting them from punishment; but I was peremptory as to them, as well as every other who, I could find, had been influenced by them, from the time they came in contact with me, and he then gave up the point; insisting, however, that the crown lawyers should have the benefit of their evidence, if they chose to become witnesses. I told him I had no doubt they would procure M'Lachlan's evidence, such as it was; with Campbell, I assured him they would have more difficulty; but it was a matter which must be decided by the parties themselves, in which I would not at all interfere.

Warrants were issued for the apprehension of a great number more; and so little attention was paid to the accuracy of the information, and so much anxiety was shown to increase the apparent magnitude of the confederacy, that, in the confusion of the first few days, several were arrested who had no connexion whatever with it. I knew not how far many of them were implicated, but by remonstrating against them proceeding upon loose and general information, I prevented a number from being taken into custody; which also caused an investigation into the cases of those who had been wrongfully accused, and they were immediately set at liberty. The sheriff depute of the county had nominally the management, but Mr. Reddie virtually conducted the whole official details, and to that gentleman's humane attention to every mitigating circumstance, I must bear the strongest testimony. He evinced the greatest solicitude, that no person should suffer who was not seriously implicated, and was always ready to give weight to everything that could in the smallest degree palliate the conduct or ameliorate the sufferings of those who were involved. Many of their families were in the greatest penury, and I strongly enforced the necessity of making provision for them; when Mr. Reddie immediately applied to the magistrates, who granted them a regular allowance from the public subscription, and additional sums were privately given in cases of the greatest necessity and hardship.

Although the crown lawyers had no evidence to bring any one to trial, but what could be elicited from accessaries, they were not long in obtaining their desire with respect to those they had already in custody, and also every other who had taken part in, or had any knowledge of, the confederacy. M'Lachlan*, as I had predicted, was the first who

* This man's conduct was too contemptible to deserve attention, were it not for the importance subsequently attached to his statements by a certain party, on which account it may be alleged I have an interest in blackening his character; but to answer all cavils of that nature, I will state a few incontrovertible facts. At the time the confederacy commenced, *he belonged* to the local militia, had of course taken the oath of allegiance, and was some time on permanent duty during its continuance. He bound himself to keep everything connected with that confederacy *secret*, and told me *all he knew, and something more.* Although I did not know it till afterwards, it was he who furnished the written copy of the oath produced in the House of Commons, which he wrote from memory, where he said it was *too deeply impressed* ever to be effaced. When the parties were apprehended, he was the first to give information, and was the cause of a number of others being taken into custody. He became a witness for the crown, against his colleagues, and when before the court, upon his oath, *could not recollect* a sentence of the oath he had furnished, upon which the charge chiefly rested. He then made an affidavit, charging me with being the author of the whole plot; which raised him finally to the rank of a patriot and a martyr. Upon this man's authority, the editor of a newspaper, in Glasgow, founded charges and published libels against me, which have done me incalculable injury; and by the false impression they produced upon the public mind, have been se-

made disclosures. He informed upon every person he knew, and offered to become a witness without reservation; and as the examination proceeded, several others following his example, the crown lawyers soon became confident of being able to establish their case. In consequence of these new informations, I was for two or three weeks constantly occupied, in endeavouring to prevent the apprehension of others, or interceding for those to be set at liberty whom they caused to be taken into custody*. I was, myself, among the first against whom M'Lachlan gave information, as having a knowledge of their proceedings, and (as I had anticipated) the course of the examinations, together with my not being taken into custody, immediately caused a suspicion, which, as soon as the precognitions were closed and an

riously prejudicial to the interest of society. He is more indebted to my forbearance than his own prudence, that he has not been sent before a jury to answer for his conduct; for the libels have long ago been submitted to the most eminent counsel at the bar, (of opposite political opinions,) who have none of them any doubt as to the issue. For his conduct there can be no excuse; he could not have seen the man twice without finding there was no credit to be attached to his statements, yet he thought him a fit subject for a protegée.

* In consequence of these informations, a person was apprehended, in whose house I had resided for some time, and who had shown me great hospitality, when I was in difficulties, on my return from Ireland, at the end of 1813, and I have been accused of basely requiting his kindness, by giving information against him. It is only necessary, however, to examine the declarations of M'Kinlay, in the account of his Trial, afterwards published at Edinburgh, to ascertain from whom the information was received. The fact was, the moment I heard he was involved, I did everything in my power to get him set at liberty; but was only able to prevent him from being sent to Edinburgh and put upon his trial; and had I not so interfered, from the greater respectability of his situation in life, he would have been one of the first selected. Had he been even indirectly tampered with by any of the parties with whom I came in contact, I would at once have peremptorily insisted upon his discharge.

intercourse allowed with their friends, was disseminated and extended abroad.

In consequence of the crown lawyers being precluded from proceeding against Campbell, and the view entertained of his general character, they were exceedingly anxious to get him to become a witness. Every method they could think of was resorted to, to induce him to confess; but, although he was aware several of the others had made disclosures, he would make no admission whatever; and, in this situation, he was sent to Edinburgh Castle with those they intended to bring to trial. As the circumstances connected with this man's becoming a witness for the crown are both curious and important, I shall distinctly relate what came within my knowledge, which, in a great measure, confirms the statement he made before the High Court of Justiciary. It was believed he had a knowledge of some particular facts which they had not arrived at, respecting the persons who had promised to assist them with money for the delegation to England, which, together with his general character and deportment, made them attach great importance to the evidence they believed he could give. They kept him ignorant of my having secured him from being brought to trial, and the sheriff of the county and Mr. Salmon, then temporarily acting as procurator fiscal*, plied him in various ways; but neither a threatened trial, nor general promises, had any effect. After the prisoners were removed to Edinburgh, Campbell remained for some time equally inflexible and unbending, and repeated references were made to me for my opinion and assistance, to

* This gentleman had been partially intrusted in the preliminary part of the proceedings, in consequence of my suggesting him as the medium for employing another person. For his share in the business, he got confirmed in the situation, (which he still holds,) which appointment would otherwise not have taken place.

overcome his scruples. I, however, positively refused to interfere, informing them that, from all I had seen, they might depend upon anything he did communicate, but that I would do nothing to influence him. I was then asked, what effect I considered offering him a situation under government was likely to produce; but I could only refer to the general character I had given, and was told they would try that experiment. I had no means of knowing personally the manner in which they ultimately succeeded, but Mr. Drummond informed me, a considerable time before Campbell made his statement, that they had offered him a place in the Excise, which he rejected; and that he, at last, consented, on their agreeing to furnish him with the means of going to the continent. The account Mr. Drummond gave me varied in no essential particular from that given by Campbell, which I believe was substantially correct, and from other circumstances, within my own knowledge, the statement he made respecting Mr. Salmon threatening him at Glasgow, I believe to have been equally true. I cannot state positively whether Campbell did or did not contemplate, in the first instance, to deceive the crown lawyers, by entering into this agreement, for the purpose of invalidating his evidence; but I am rather inclined to believe, it was an afterthought, arising out of the long delay, and the opportunity he had of communicating indirectly with his associates, who were to be tried. My reason for thinking so is this: when he agreed to become a witness, he drew out a very full statement, in writing, of all their transactions, for the crown lawyers; and it was he gave the information that Mr. Kerr* was

* I was personally acquainted with this gentleman, who was in a respectable situation in life: unobtrusive and inoffensive in his manners, his deficiency of general knowledge of the world and of society, had inadvertently led him into this imprudent connexion.

the person who had promised to procure the money for the Carlisle delegation, who was immediately apprehended, on a Justiciary warrant.

The crown lawyers, believing they had got sufficient evidence to establish their case, two of the parties were indicted, to stand trial on the 10th of April. The statute, upon which these indictments were laid, was passed in the fifty-second year of the late King, and is entitled, " An Act to render more effectual an Act passed in the thirty-seventh of the same reign, for preventing the administration, or taking unlawful oaths;" and, to render the case clear and distinct, I *shall* transcribe the clauses upon which the charge was founded; which are as follow:

" It is, inter alia, enacted, that every person who shall, in any manner, or form whatsoever, administer, or cause to be administered, or be aiding or assisting at the administering of any oath or engagement, purporting, or intending to bind the person taking the same to commit any treason, or murder, or any felony, punishable by law with death, shall, on conviction thereof, by due course of law, be adjudged guilty of felony, and suffer death as a felon, without benefit of clergy." And further, by section fourth of said act, it is enacted, "that persons, aiding and assisting at the administering of any such oath, or engagement, as aforesaid, and persons causing any such oath or engagement to be administered, though not present at the administering thereof,

From the representations I made of his character, he was very soon liberated on bail, and never further troubled. Had I not interfered, in all probability, he would have been retained in custody, under the operation of the suspension bill, although it had not been intended to bring him to trial. His case was noticed in the House of Commons, but was not pressed, in consequence of the member who brought it up coming to a more accurate knowledge of the facts.

shall be deemed principal offenders, and shall be tried as such, and, on conviction thereof, by due course of law, shall be adjudged guilty of felony, and shall suffer death, as felons, without benefit of clergy; although the person, or persons, who actually administered such oath or engagement, if any such there shall be, shall not have been tried or convicted." And by section sixth, it is enacted, "that every engagement or obligation whatsoever, in the nature of an oath, purporting or intending to bind the person taking the same, to commit any treason or murder, or any felony, punishable by law with death, shall be deemed an oath within the intent and meaning of this act, in whatever form or manner the same shall be administered or taken, and whether the same shall be actually administered by any person or persons, to any other person or persons, or taken by any other person or persons, without any administration thereof, by any other person or persons."

Under this statute, the indictments charged the parties with felony, with an intention to commit treason, by entering into an engagement to subvert the established government and laws, in attempting to obtain, by physical force and violent means, universal suffrage and annual parliaments; so that, by proving the felony, it constituted, constructively, an overt act of treason. No conviction had previously taken place under this statute. The novelty of the case, the form of drawing out the indictment, making one capital crime a proof of another, together with the poverty of the parties accused, and a belief of the utter inadequacy of their means seriously to affect the government, aroused the attention of the bar, and seven or eight of the most eminent counsel, for talent and character, gratuitously offered their services, to make a bold and determined stand on the relevancy of the indictment*. Every argument that profound legal knowledge and ingenuity could adduce was brought forward against the form of the proceeding; and the court, after hearing pleadings on both sides, judging it of too much importance to decide upon *viva voce* arguments, ordered printed informations, and adjourned the trial.

From the 22d of February, when the men were taken into custody, my situation had been agonising in the extreme. The most malignant demon could not have desired to make me suffer more. While I was strenuously exerting myself in every possible manner in favour of the accused, and condemning the principle of the whole proceedings against them, I was denounced as an emissary of the government, and the instigator of the whole. A thousand absurd and even contradictory reports were whispered and circulated to my prejudice, and, however inconsistent, were all credited. I was importuned by my friends to adopt some method of refuting those unfounded calumnies, but was obliged to evade their questions, or remain impenetrably silent; and, in a short time, the feeling

* Just and wholesome laws are not of more importance to society than their proper administration, and the first requisite to accomplish that object, is to secure for the accused an impartial trial. Aside from party questions, (which this may perhaps be considered) it is impossible to omit mentioning the eminently disinterested conduct, which has, of late years, distinguished the gentlemen of the Scotch bar, in encountering the two greatest enemies to justice, poverty and ignorance, on the part of the accused. In all cases affecting public liberty or of individual oppression, they have voluntarily offered their services without money and without price; nor does this alone apply to men of second-rate talent, or the young aspirants wishing to force themselves into notice, but to men of the first abilities and best-established practice, which is more, I am afraid, than can be said for their brethren in England. In the metropolis, indeed, the periodical press makes up a part of the deficiency, and relatively the account may stand thus: In Scotland the bar is everything, and the press (till very lately, and yet with few exceptions) comparatively nothing; in the metropolis, the press is everything, and the bar nothing without money.

excited was so strong, and the prejudice so deeply rooted, that no explanation or justification would have been listened to, or become available, admitting I had been in a condition to make it. My remaining in Glasgow for a considerable time, without having anything ostensible to do, gave an appearance of truth to many of these reports.

When I closed my engagement with Mr. Owen, I informed Mr. Jeffrey that I should experience some difficulty in winding up my business, and fitting out my establishment at New Lanark in the manner I could wish, in consequence of having a considerable quantity of goods on hand, which I could not for sometime turn into money, without considerable loss, and also accounts lying out which would require time to collect. Mr. Jeffrey wrote me in reply, that he fully approved of my engagement, and any accommodation I might require was at my service. He had at the time to go to London on professional business, and some delay took place before he remitted me; but I immediately commenced my preparations, and early in February sent a considerable portion of my furniture to New Lanark. I put my goods in a train of being sold, and from that period my warehouse was nearly shut up. When Mr. Owen went to London, it was agreed that I should go to Lanark, as soon as I could conveniently get away; but a short time after I received intimation, that he did not wish me to remove until his return, which, contrary to his expectation, was protracted to the middle of April; and I determined to remain in Glasgow until his arrival, and inform him of all the particulars that had occurred.

When I found it would be impossible to prevent some of the parties from being brought to trial, and that it was resolved to proceed against them capitally, I determined, if they succeeded in getting a conviction, and all my private remonstrances proved unavailing, to publish the whole proceedings, which I calculated would arrest the execution of their sentence. Beyond that period I was not pledged to be silent, and I had a short statement of facts prepared, which would immediately have appeared; an incident, however, occurred, by which I expected to be able to do it more effectually. I formerly mentioned, that the trial of two of the parties was fixed for the 10th of April, and, late in the evening of the 9th, a citation was left at my house, to appear on the trial, at Edinburgh, next morning, as an exculpatory evidence. I never have been able to learn the real intention of this measure, on the part of the prisoners, but it occurred to me that, in consequence of the reports circulated, that I was in connexion with government, it was intended to take advantage of my absence, under an impression that the shortness of the notice would put it out of my power to be present, to charge me with being an instigator; or, perhaps, if I was seriously implicated, that I should not dare to make my appearance at all. To prevent any advantage of this kind, early next morning, I posted to Edinburgh, and was in sufficient time to have appeared, admitting the trial had not been postponed. From that time to the final close of the proceedings, I expected to be put into the witness-box, on the part of the prisoners, which would have given me an opportunity of laying open the whole case to the country, without doing any injury to them, as I could not have spoken to a particular fact respecting any of them. No situation could have been more favourable for eliciting the truth. Mr. Jeffrey and Mr. Cockburn were two of the counsel for the prisoners, and did not then know how I was connected with the transactions;

but as they knew all my previous history, it would have given every advantage for completely sifting my evidence. I could easily have been brought forward as a witness for the crown, had I been disposed to support the interest of the prosecution; but the mere fact of appearing upon that side, under any circumstances, would have impugned my motives and thrown discredit upon every asseveration I might make.

Mr. Finlay had been some time gone, to attend his duty in parliament, and, on going to Edinburgh, I got an introduction from Mr. Reddie to the Lord Advocate, and called upon him, on the evening of the 10th, after the trial had been postponed. I found him in company with the Solicitor General and Henry Home Drummond, Esq. the depute advocate, who was conducting the prosecutions; and, as it was the first time I had come in personal contact with any of the crown lawyers, I embraced the opportunity of strongly urging the impolicy and impropriety of their measures; I told them, that the promise made to me, not to interfere, had been broken at the very time I felt confident of being able to dissipate the confederacy, which would have had a much better moral effect upon the people's minds; that the men were too contemptible to create any serious alarm, or be made the subjects of capital punishment by a government so strong and secure as that of Great Britain; and I pressed them, by all means, to depart from the capital charge, the prosecuting of which would only produce greater irritation and resistance, and bring discredit on the government. My observations seemed to strike them with considerable force, particularly when I described the means I had of breaking up the confederacy, and the circumstances under which the persons had been taken into custody; but the Lord Advocate seemed deeply imbued with the opinion, that it was necessary for him to establish his case, and felt perfectly confident of a conviction, as soon as the legal difficulties were surmounted.

Mr. Owen returned from London on the 16th of April, and on the 18th I met him at New Lanark, and informed him precisely how matters stood. On arriving, he had heard the reports circulated, and the extent of the prejudice which prevailed; and, on learning the dilemma in which I was placed, and viewing the difficulties that stood in the way of removing the impression, he considered that it destroyed all hope of me enjoying comfort at New Lanark, or of being useful in promoting his designs there. It was a part of his plan, in his endeavours to ameliorate the condition of the labouring population, *not to identify himself with any political party;* and, although he expressed himself perfectly satisfied with the rectitude of my intentions, he conceived it necessary to avoid giving any ground of suspicion. He therefore considered it better to give up the idea of my going to New Lanark, and await the result of his efforts in England, where narrow prejudices did not so much prevail, and in the mean time to make me some compensation for the loss of time and expenses I had been subjected to. Previous to Mr. Owen's arrival in Scotland, I had formed precisely the same opinion, and anticipated every view he had taken; and, two days before I met him at New Lanark, I had removed my family to Edinburgh, where I immediatlely proceeded, determined there to await the result of the trials which I calculated would bring my case to a crisis. I must ever regret that any thing should have occurred to prevent me from participating in the labours of this amiable and benevolent gentleman. My friends were all of opinion my humble efforts would have been useful, in ascertaining how far the theory he has promulgated was reducible to practice, and the pursuit would have been perfectly consonant to my own mind. Mr. Owen's known character, the nature of the pursuit, and its being unallied with the theory of any political party in the country, might have allayed distrust until time afforded an opportunity for explanation. Many men will however avow their sentiments on abstract principles, although opposed to preconceived opinion and prejudice, but few feel sufficient interest, or have sufficient stamina, to make the same avowal respecting individual acts of a similar kind, although convinced of the virtuous intention of the actor.

My sensations, on arriving in Edinburgh, can more easily be conceived than described. I saw every tie that previously bound me to society was rent asunder. Having to depend exclusively upon my own exertions for success in life, I saw the hopes I had reasonably entertained, from the connexions I had formed, blasted and scattered to the winds. I was aware of the confirmation that would be given to the surmises already made, by the line of conduct I was obliged to pursue, and that my future justification depended upon many contingent events, the result of which I could not foresee. I saw I was in a great measure thrown upon the mercy of men who knew nothing of me personally, and who (I had reason to be afraid, and have since fatally experienced) had not the means, or were incapable of appreciating my motives. I was without a single friend to consult. Mr. Jeffrey and Mr. Cockburn were near me, but with them I could not communicate, without forfeiting the promise I had made, which I was determined not to do, whatever I might suffer. One link only, in the chain of my former connexions, remained unbroken, in the person of a friend in

Glasgow, whom I made acquainted with all the circumstances. Through his medium my future correspondence was to be kept up with Messrs. Finlay and Reddie, and I authorised him to dispose of my effects; including those I had provided for fitting out my establishment at New Lanark, which were sold under one-third of their value.

The Lord Advocate withdrew the indictments upon which informations had been ordered, and preferred another in what he considered an amended form, but without departing from the original principle. The trial on this second indictment came on, on the 19th of May, but the relevancy was again strenuously disputed; and, after another long debate, the Court declared themselves still dissatisfied, and repeated their order for printed informations. A third indictment preferred met with a similar fate. Printed informations had at last to be given in, which protracted the time until the middle of July, when the Court gave their decision on the points of law, finding the indictment relevant, and appointed the 19th of that month for proceeding with the trial.

During the three months which these discussions occupied, I remained at Edinburgh in a state of great anxiety. I had frequent communications with the crown lawyers, and embraced every opportunity of restating my former arguments, urging them to confine the case to the minor charge, which would only involve an arbitrary punishment. Mr. Reddie had always been of opinion, that the capital charge should never have been preferred, and on the 20th of June, Mr. Finlay attacked the Lord Advocate in the House of Commons, accusing him of imbecility in conducting the legal proceedings; and affirming that, by his misconduct, the men would escape punishment altogether. This attack forced the Lord Advocate to post immediately to London, to defend himself in the House, and during his absence, I had various interviews with the Solicitor General and Mr. Drummond, who both became convinced of the propriety of restricting the libel; and, on the Lord Advocate's return, it was agreed that, as soon as the Court, by its decision, established the point of law, the capital part of the charge should be withdrawn. Other events had occurred in the interim, which no doubt contributed to induce them to adopt that resolution. The case which the ministry had chiefly depended upon, in England, as a ground of justification for passing the Suspension Bill, had entirely failed, from their anxiety to magnify the amount of the danger and the extent of the crime committed. Watson, whose case was to decide the principle as well as the fate of his colleagues, had been put upon his trial for High Treason, on the 9th of June, but from the total inadequacy of their means to commit the crime charged, the jury acquitted him; while it has been admitted, on all hands, if the party had been arraigned for a misdemeanor only, the same jury would have found them guilty. Oliver, the avowed emissary of the Home Secretary, had been denounced by the Leeds Mercury, on the 10th of June; and in the report of the Secret Committee of the House of Lords on the 12th, made for the purpose of justifying the renewal of the Suspension Bill, it was distinctly admitted that he, and others employed by the magistracy, had directly instigated the people to commit the crimes they had been engaged to detect or prevent. The current of popular feeling had set strongly against the internal policy of the ministry; and even their regular supporters began to consider they had been taken by surprise, and that the amount of the danger had been greatly exaggerated. These circumstances, together with the determined opposition they had met from the opposite side of the bar, lowered the tone of the crown lawyers of Scotland, although they still entertained no doubt of obtaining a conviction, when they proceeded to the merits of the case.

A few days after my arrival in Edinburgh, I wrote to the agents for the prisoners in Glasgow, informing them, that I probably might have occasion soon to leave Scotland; but if the prisoners, or their legal advisers, considered my presence useful for their defence, I would remain to give them the benefit of my evidence, and requested them to let me know their opinion without delay. No notice was taken of this intimation, and I was in some difficulty to know how to proceed; but, after viewing the case in all its bearings, I resolved to remain and await the course of events, instructing my friend in Glasgow instantly to apprise me if any inquiry was made after me. Nothing further transpired, until two days previous to the trial, when inquiries were made by the agents for the prisoners in every direction in Glasgow, and a hue and cry raised, that I was nowhere to be found. On receiving this information, I gave directions that the agents at Glasgow should be furnished with my address; and being afraid that intimation might be too late to enable them to cite me as a witness, and to put it out of their power to set up any such pretext, I wrote directly to the agent for the defence in Edinburgh. On the evening of the 18th of July, the night previous to the trial, I was waited upon by Mr. Gibson, writer to the signet, a gentleman who had taken a warm interest on the part of the prisoners, for the purpose of ascertaining what I knew, before they would venture to call me as a witness. I told him they must have had some specific design in view, when they summoned me in the former instance; that, if they considered I could have been of service then, I was aware of no circumstance which could alter the case now; that I was certainly well acquainted with every particular connected with the transactions; and, if it was *their* wish or design to enable the country to form a correct opinion, they would have an opportunity of doing so, by putting me into the witness-box; that it was *my* most anxious desire the public should be fully informed of every fact, and I only wished an opportunity of making known the whole truth, without partiality to any party; but in consequence of the rumours that had gone abroad respecting me, (of which he could not be ignorant,) I would not say one word until I was before the Court. I further added, that what I could state I considered would operate materially in favour of the prisoners, and could not possibly injure them, as I did not even know them personally; and that my anxiety to see them acquitted could not be surpassed by their own. A lengthened conversation ensued. Mr. Gibson ineffectually exhausted all his ingenuity to elicit the particulars, and concluded by informing me, that, under the circumstances, they could not hazard my evidence; that, from what was formerly known of my principles, he did not believe I had any intention to injure the prisoners, and he gave me full credit for the anxiety I felt upon their account; but that they had a certain line of defence agreed upon, which they confidently believed would prove successful; and, were they to bring me forward as a witness, my statement would possibly *interfere with their plan.* Thus, because a statement of facts would not promote the view of either party, was I deprived of the opportunity of laying open the case to the country, which would have prevented many of the misconceptions that followed. Next morning (19th July) the trial of Andrew M'Kinlay, the first person selected, came on before the High Court of Justiciary *. The crown lawyers had the greatest confidence in Campbell establishing their case, and as soon as some preliminary objections brought forward by the counsel for the prisoner had been overruled by the Court, he was introduced as the leading witness. After being sworn, the customary question in the Scotch Court was put to him by the Judge; viz.: if he had received any reward, or promise of reward, for giving his evidence, when, to the astonishment of every one, (except the *prisoner's* counsel,) he answered, *that he had.* The presiding Judge cautioned him, that he was now in no parallel situation with the pannel; and that it was not competent to subject him to prosecution for any concern he may have had in the transactions, after being adduced as a witness, as long as he adhered to the truth. Campbell replied, he was perfectly conscious of the situation in which he was placed, and proceeded to give a minute detail of the circumstances that had occurred between him and the crown lawyers, at his different examinations. He gave a full account of the threats and promises held out to him, and concluded by stating, that the promise made to defray the expense of his going to the Continent, he considered still a subsisting engagement. The counsel for the defence insisted on

* Before the jury was impanneled, the Lord Advocate stated, that one of the objects he had in view had been accomplished, the court having settled the law, by finding the indictment relevant; which he trusted would oppose a barrier against the commission of the crime in future; and, in that reliance, under all the circumstances, he would restrict the indictment, to infer only an arbitrary punishment.

calling the parties alluded to, to corroborate Campbell's testimony, which was also agreed to by the Lord Advocate; but the Court objected to their examination, on the ground that, whether he had correctly or incorrectly stated the circumstances, he was altogether inadmissible as a witness. The crown lawyers had reposed so much confidence on Campbell's bringing the charge directly home to the prisoner, that they were completely taken by surprise, and paralysed in the subsequent part of the proof. Their case depended on their being able to establish the *purport* and *administration* of the oath or obligation charged in the indictment; but the law of evidence did not allow them to read it over in connexion to the witnesses. The indictment was also very inaccurately drawn; the specification of the acts done at one time and place, and by one party, were transposed and charged against another; and the counsel for the prisoner were too cautious and vigilant to allow any latitude in putting questions beyond the limits of the specifications. M Lachlan and three more of the accessaries were successively brought forward as witnesses, but they all swore they could not remember one connected sentence of the oath or obligation they had taken; and the crown lawyers, restricted by their own specifications, were prevented from putting questions to prove its administration. The Lord Advocate then stated, that the testimony the witnesses had given was very different from what he had expected from their precognitions, and as he could not produce any more conclusive evidence, however much he might regret such a result, the prisoner was entitled to a verdict of acquittal. The jury accordingly returned a unanimous verdict, finding the libel not proven.

Thus terminated the case, in Scotland, upon

which the ministry depended for a justification of their proceedings; and, as the propriety of their policy was equally questionable as it had been in England, they also met with as signal a defeat. As the circumstances which led to this unexpected conclusion, on the part of the crown lawyers, are a little curious, I will relate them, as they afterwards came to my knowledge.

I formerly stated, for some time after the men were taken into custody, and while the panic and terror of the consequences continued to operate, a number of them had unreservedly disclosed every particular. There were, indeed, only two or three exceptions among the whole party; for, as the crown lawyers only wanted a certain number to become witnesses, they had frequently to warn the others, not to make admissions which might militate against themselves, as they could give them no assurance they would not be brought to trial. Even M'Kinlay, more than once, offered to disclose all and become a witness; and there can be no doubt, had the trials been brought on when the examinations were concluded, a number of them would have been convicted. The long delay, caused by the discussions on the relevancy, gave them time to reflect, and the list of witnesses, with the first indictment, showed clearly there was no evidence to produce a conviction but from amongst themselves. When they were removed to Edinburgh Castle, the witnesses were kept separate from those intended to be brought to trial; but, for the benefit of air and exercise, they were allowed to get out on the ramparts, at intervals, under the charge of sentinels, where many opportunities occurred of eluding their vigilance, and holding communications with each other. The counsel for the defence were excluded from access to the witnesses, but had regular admission to those who were indicted, and the weak parts of the prosecutor's case came to be discovered and pointed out. On discovering those weak parts, it would as naturally occur, that there was no law to punish a man for the loss of his memory; and the popular odium attached to a *sociis criminis* becoming a witness, and the sympathy and feeling for their confederates, were a strong inducement to make them drink of the Lethean stream. Whether Campbell originally intended the trick played off upon the crown lawyers, or not, can only be known to himself, and I have already given my opinion on that point. At all events, the want of recollection in him would have but ill accorded with his general character; and the method he had recourse to was equally effectual in saving his associate. After he agreed to become a witness, he was allowed considerable indulgence, and when he had taken his resolution, he wrote a detailed account of his communications with the crown lawyers, and the promises made to him, before he would agree to give his evidence. This statement he secretly inclosed, in a roll of tobacco, which he sent as a present to M'Kinlay, who immediately put it into the hands of his counsel, who kept it a profound secret, until Campbell was put into the witness-box. The crown lawyers had not the most distant suspicion; and his answer to the interrogatory, "if he had received any reward, or promise of reward, for giving his evidence," utterly astounded them, coming upon them like their death knell. Nothing could be managed with more address. Mr. Jeffrey, on the part of the prisoner, objected to his being received as a witness, on the ground of being refused access to ascertain his character, and a lengthened discussion ensued, before the court overruled the objection; the crown lawyers insisting that he should, and the counsel for the defence, that he should not, be allowed to give evidence.

When I called upon the crown lawyers, next day, to learn the particulars of the trial, they appeared like chagrin and mortification personified*. The dreadful situation in which it had left me, by affording me no opportunity for explanation, was sufficient to absorb all my attention; yet the very awkward appearance they made, the sense of shame and the soreness they felt, at their complete discomfiture, produced in my mind a mixed feeling of pity and gratification; pity, that they should have exposed themselves, in such a manner, by pursuing an erroneous system of policy; and gratification that the men had escaped. I pointed out to the Lord Advocate the superior effect it would have produced upon the minds of the people, had I been allowed to proceed with my plan, to induce them to give up their foolish project of their own accord; and that the best amends which could now be made, would be immediately to liberate all who were in custody. He said, he might be justified in detaining them under the Habeas Corpus Act Suspension Bill, but he now viewed the matter in the same light which I had represented it, in consequence of which he had made up his mind to liberate them all, without delay. He admitted they had acted on a wrong principle, but that the blame was not, in the first instance, attributable to him, but to the local authorities of Glasgow, who had taken the people into custody without orders. He then went on to state, that, on his arrival in London,

* Mr. Drummond attributed their failure to a want of management, in not, in the first instance, making sure of evidence, to produce a conviction. On the conversation turning upon the means adopted to break up the organizations formed during the administration of Mr. Pitt, he, with a strong emphasis, remarked, "had the case depended upon the late Lord Melville, *he* would not have drawn a trigger until he was sure to kill."

in February, while the Secret Committees were sitting, he represented that a perfect knowledge had been obtained of the proceedings of the confederacy at Glasgow; that measures were in progress, which he sanguinely hoped would induce the people to abandon it, and, in the meantime, if any disposition was shown to disturb the public peace, information would be received in sufficient time, to take the necessary precautions to prevent or counteract the attempt; that, in consequence of this representation, it had been agreed, that no interference should take place, unless there was an *actual and immediate* danger of their breaking out into open disturbance; that an order, to that effect, was sent to the Solicitor General in Edinburgh, who transmitted it to Glasgow, and that the first account he received was, that the men had been apprehended at the meeting on the 22d; that a statement of the reasons for taking them into custody had been afterwards transmitted, which was considered satisfactory, and accounted for the subsequent proceedings; but that the statement made to me, respecting the order being peremptory, *was not true*, it being altogether conditional. I had always entertained strong suspicions on this point, and had ineffectually endeavoured to arrive at the truth, until the mortification and disappointment of the Lord Advocate induced him to relate the above particulars, which, as far as the nature of the order went, were confirmed by the Solicitor General*.

On referring to the other events which occurred at the same time, the reader will perhaps be

* I afterwards ascertained the true state of the case; none of the magistrates of the city of Glasgow were consulted; five persons only were present at the deliberation, and there was a difference of opinion, even among them, as to the propriety of taking the men into custody. I could give the names of the parties, as well as the manner each of them voted, but it might appear invidious.

able to discover a reason for the minister being easily satisfied with the statement in justification of the contravention of his order, without considering it necessary to institute an inquiry into its accuracy. I have related the facts, and other persons can judge for themselves. It occurs to me, however, that it would be no way injurious to the interest of society, were it more frequently known whether acts of this kind are the consequence of orders emanating directly from the office of the Home Secretary, or are the spontaneous productions of the local authorities, when they conceive it may answer the purpose of the minister, and secure his approbation.

A more accurate estimate can be formed of human character and of the scope of a design, when we have an opportunity of judging of the emotions, as they successively arise in the mind, in the various stages of its progress, than when we link together a great many circumstances, and judge of them as a whole. Events frequently occur in the course of execution, so minute as to escape observation, although of sufficient importance to produce a result very different from what was intended; yet that result may be of such a nature as to render it difficult to discover whether it was an original conception of the actor or not, by which means we are frequently deceived in the estimate we form of individual as well as general character. As I had frequent opportunities of unreservedly hearing the sentiments of the crown lawyers during the progress of the trial, I will state the impression produced on my mind, as to the original intention of the measures pursued. Had, they, in the first instance, succeeded in establishing the administration of the oath, (of which they entertained no doubt,) two or three would have been sentenced to capital punishment, and a number more to transportation; and had the circumstances which I have related not intervened, I have no hesitation in saying, their sentences would have been carried into execution. The expected severity of the punishment, I believe, had considerable influence in preventing a conviction, even at the end; for the accomplices were ignorant of the libel having been restricted, and gave their evidence under an impression, that if their associates were found guilty, they would be capitally convicted. Singular as it may appear, this intention was not the result of any impression on the mind of the Lord Advocate, that such a punishment was necessary as an example, in reference to the state of society in Scotland, or in consequence of the moral turpitude of the parties accused; for, as soon as I had an opportunity of personally representing their condition, and the true nature of the case, the crown lawyers individually felt strongly for their situation. From my observations, after I made these representations, I have reason to believe, if it had depended upon the Lord Advocate, the prosecutions would not have been persisted in; but such was not the policy of the period; and nothing can more clearly illustrate the impotence and subserviency of an officer removable at pleasure, although nominally possessing the most extensive powers of any in Britain. I do not believe that, for a long period, any Lord Advocate of Scotland has been so anxious to obtain popularity as the present Lord Meadowbank*; although from the state of

* A proof of this was his granting a poll election to the borough of Montrose; but as soon as the ministry saw the consequences likely to result from the precedent, they obliged him to refuse the same privilege to Aberdeen, where it was admitted (even by the magistrates) malversations had taken place to a great extent; which those who were ignorant of the controlling power exercised over him, considered an evidence of inconsistency.

the times, and being counteracted in his designs, none have been more unsuccessful or more generally censured, as an enemy to popular rights. In conducting those state prosecutions, the crown lawyers displayed comparatively little ability, but I never saw any appearance of vindictive feeling*: it must also be borne in mind that a more powerful array of talent was brought forward against them than, perhaps, ever appeared in any similar case in this country.

With the most perfect openness and candour, when I first met the Lord Advocate, I explicitly informed him of the nature of my former connexions; and that, agreeable to the stipulations with Messrs. Finlay and Reddie, all my friends, who felt any interest on my account, should be made fully acquainted with the whole transaction, whatever might be their political opinions. The only alleviating circumstance, to counterbalance the disappointment I felt at losing the opportunity of explaining on the trial, arose from the consideration, that there was no longer any restraint in opening that communication.

As soon, therefore, as the trial was concluded, I wrote to Mr. Jeffrey, and, without entering into any explanation, requested him to form no definite opinion on the ex-parte statements or rumours that had reached him, but to suspend his judgment until he had an opportunity of learning the facts. That from the natural tendency in human nature to represent our own actions in the most favourable light, he might consider it was with a view to excite his feelings in my favour, were I to enter into particulars; I therefore begged to refer him

* As a proof of the personal feeling of the Lord Advocate, it consists with my knowledge, that M'Kinlay called upon him after his acquittal, to return thanks for his treatment during his imprisonment, when the Lord Advocate presented him with money to bear his expenses home, and assist his family after his return.

to Mr. Finlay, Mr. Reddie, and the Lord Advocate for a full account of everything that had occurred. Mr. Jeffrey stated, in answer, that although he had felt much hurt at the reports which had reached him, from what he had formerly known of me, he had no reason to believe I would not give a faithful representation of my conduct; and, at all events, before he made a reference to other persons, he wished to see me personally. This led to several long conferences with Mr. Jeffrey, and afterwards with Mr. Cockburn; when I circumstantially related every event as it had taken place. Many of the statements made to them were gross fabrications*; others, that had some foundation in truth, had been so completely distorted, as rendered it difficult to discover their connexion with the events to which they related; but all of them I fully and satisfactorily explained; I, however, insisted on their referring to all the other parties, to satisfy themselves of the truth. The Lord Advocate had offered to give Mr. Jeffrey, or any of my friends, every explanation they might require; and that he was ready to bear testimony to the honourable manner I had conducted myself in all my communications with him. Mr. Jeffrey, however, declined making that reference, but he soon after met Messrs. Finlay and Reddie for the purpose, who fully satisfied him, (if he previously entertained any doubt,) that I had given a correct representation of the facts.

Fully conscious of the difficulty of my situation, I had looked forward to this explanation with the greatest anxiety. Those only can form an adequate conception of my feelings, who

* Among other forgeries it was asserted, I had given out that I was encouraged by Mr. Jeffrey, to organize and foment a conspiracy, for the purpose of overthrowing the government.

have had the experience of conjoining a consciousness of having acted right to a conviction of the difficulty of convincing the bulk of society either that they had done so, or that they had been actuated by proper motives. In such a situation no justice is to be expected from the unthinking multitude, no candour from the partizans of a party, nor reliance to be placed on the *gratitude* of the cool, calculating, cold-blooded, heartless politician; and we turn with proportionally greater avidity and confidence to those who, having had an opportunity of obtaining a more accurate knowledge of our character, can form a juster estimate, and are therefore better able to appreciate our motives. My connexion with them had never had any reference to political objects; the services they had rendered me were wholly from personal considerations, but they had followed as a consequence from what I had suffered, by endeavouring to ameliorate the condition of the numerous population employed in the most extensive branch of manufacture in the country. They knew that, in that endeavour, I had sacrificed my private interest, my time, and ultimately my health: they knew that when government unwisely interfered, I had suffered severely by a prosecution which I might easily have averted, had I been influenced by personal considerations: in fine, their knowledge of my conduct, character and principles, for years, was the chief ground upon which I could confidently appeal to their judgment, when circumstances had placed me in a situation where my sense of duty induced me to throw myself into a breach which, in that instance, had in some measure identified me with that very government, the general tendency of whose measures I disapproved.

Being therefore indebted to personal character

alone for my connexions, I had every inducement not to wantonly sacrifice that character; and no stronger evidence can be given of the opinion I entertained of the correctness of my conduct, in assisting the government to preserve the public peace, than that the two gentlemen, to whom I specifically referred, were as well known and distinguished for their political opinions being opposed to those of the existing administration, as for their honourable and upright character in public and private life. It may be alleged, that the reference made to them was in their capacity of private friends or patrons; and that, having no public or political relation, I take an unwarrantable liberty in giving publicity to their opinions; but to this I would answer, that the positive stipulation which I made, that they should be so referred to, belongs as much to the public as any other part of the transaction, and their opinions have had so much influence over my subsequent measures, that to do justice to myself, imperious necessity compels me to state everything without reserve.

On learning the particulars, Mr. Jeffrey declared his perfect conviction, that there was no ground for throwing the slightest imputation on the motives which had induced me to act as I had done; that, although I had been prevented from carrying my plan fully into effect, he was satisfied I had rendered a very important service to society; but that the danger to which I had exposed myself, and the sacrifices I had made were so great and so completely out of the common road, resembling romance rather than reality, that it would be almost impossible, from the equivocal situation in which it had placed me, to convince the great mass of society of the purity of my motives. He therefore looked upon it as the greatest misfortune that could have befallen me, as it had severed my connexions and deprived me of the means of usefully exerting my own talents, while, it had put it out of the power of my friends to avow their sentiments, or render me any assistance in this country.

In these opinions Mr. Cockburn fully coincided; but he thought that no man was justifiable in making such a sacrifice; as, in all cases of the kind, it was difficult for the public to judge whether men were actuated by good or bad motives; that society was entitled to take its chance, rather than that an upright man should expose himself to such hazard; and, although great benefit might be derived from a good man acting in the manner I had done, it was a dangerous precedent, and liable to abuse in the hands of a bad one; that I was wrong in putting my happiness in the power of the administration or its adherents, from a belief that they were actuated by the same benevolent views as I had been myself, for, in all probability, they were incapable of drawing a line of distinction between me and the profligate, mercenary myrmidons whom, there was reason to believe, they had otherwise employed; that I might have known that, regardless of the effect it might have upon my character or feelings, they would attend no longer to any engagement they made with me than suited their crooked and mistaken policy. Both, however, declared they were so perfectly satisfied of the rectitude of my intentions, and the sacrifice I had made of my future prospects, that, whatever claim I had upon them for my former conduct, it was now greatly enhanced by my present situation; that I might, in the most unlimited manner, depend upon their influence, together with that of all their friends, to whom the matter could be communicated, being exerted in my behalf, in any way which would best promote my future comfort; but, in the excited state of the public mind, there was no hope of overcoming prejudice by a public explanation, on which account they considered they could be of no service to me, unless I left the country. They therefore proposed that I should go to the United States of America, where all their interest should be concentrated to procure me a comfortable and respectable settlement.

To that proposition, however, I had insuperable objections; my children were all very young, and ill-suited for emigration; my own health was in a precarious state, and, if any contingency deprived them of me, they would have been left in a foreign land, without their natural protector; and to go there myself, and leave them in this country, was altogether out of the question. Nor could I submit to the idea of leaving the country in a private or clandestine manner, without having an opportunity of explaining my conduct, as it would have justified the insinuations and confirmed the belief, that it was not defensible. I also considered that, as I had sacrificed everything on public grounds, government was fairly and justly entitled to indemnify me for my losses, and not leave me dependent upon private friends. Under that impression, when I became fully sensible of the effect produced by their measures, I had written Mr. Finlay pointedly, stating that opinion; and that, as he had been the cause of involving me, he was in honour bound to see me fairly indemnified. Mr. Finlay at once admitted the justice of the claim, and his own obligation to see it complied with; and a few days previous to my seeing Mr. Jeffrey, he had apprised me that, before leaving London, at the end of the session, he had an interview with

Lord Sidmouth for the purpose, and had minutely explained the nature of my situation; that his Lordship said, it was the imperative duty of government to afford me every protection, and his firm determination that full compensation should be made for what I had suffered, by so laudably lending my aid in the public service, and that provision should be made for me in any manner he (Mr. Finlay) chose to point out. The Lord Advocate had also expressed himself warmly, on the peculiar hardship of my situation. He said that, although he had no previous knowledge of me, from the manner I had acted in my intercourse with him, he had, in the whole course of his life, met with no person in whose case he had felt so much interest; and that, as a matter of personal feeling, independent of official obligation, he considered himself bound to see me get justice.

In discussing these points with Messrs. Jeffrey and Cockburn, one palpable difficulty presented itself; which was, that if I accepted a situation under government, it would confirm the opinion entertained, that I had been dishonourably connected with them from the commencement; and, with the view of obviating the objection, when Mr. Jeffrey met Mr. Finlay, he made a proposition that he should join him and his friends in some arrangement to place me in a situation independent of any connexion with government. That gentleman, however, declined making any sacrifice; assigning as a reason, that the losses I had sustained, and the services I had rendered, justly entitled government to indemnify me; that they had fully admitted their right to do so; and as there was no doubt but it would be done in a way agreeable to my own feelings, there was no necessity for my friends interfering. I had, afterwards, abundant reason to know how little dependence was to be placed on those specious promises; but, in the mean time, it was considered nothing farther could be done, until the manner they purposed to carry them into effect was ascertained.

Until after M'Kinlay's trial, the imputations against me had got little publicity beyond the district of country and circle of society where I had been personally known, and no attempt had been made to establish their authenticity but verbal rumour. The failure of the state prosecutions in both kingdoms; the questionable manner in which the guilt of the accused had been attempted to be established, created a high degree of popular excitement; and the exposure of the proceedings of Oliver at Derby and other parts of the country, which took place at the same time, were followed by a general burst of indignation, and subjected the whole internal policy of the ministry to general obloquy. During this ferment there was no time for dispassionate or impartial enquiry: one sweeping conclusion was drawn, that no person, actuated by honourable or patriotic feelings, could, in the remotest degree, be allied with such a government; on the contrary, that all the virtues were concentrated in those who most violently opposed them; without considering whether the means they employed were inimical to the preservation or extension of rational liberty, and did not furnish the chief apology for the abuses of power complained of.

It was my first impulse, before consulting any friends, when deprived of the opportunity of explaining in court, that I should publish a relation of the whole facts; and, with this view, I wrote to a person in Glasgow, with whom I had been formerly acquainted, in whose candour and judgment I imagined I could rely, requesting him to point out the circumstances which had made the deepest impression on the public mind, and would, therefore, require to be more particularly attended to. In this calculation I was, however, deceived. The popular mania had made too deep an inroad on his mind to leave room for the exercise of either judgment or discretion. The immortal honour and glory to be derived from unravelling another link in the chain of the Machiavelian policy of the minister, was too strong to be resisted: he contemplated, in prospective, the possibility of having his name indelibly inscribed on the roll of patriot fame; and against such fearful odds, friendship, professedly founded on a previous knowledge of my principles and character, was not to be balanced. To qualify himself for rising in this school of patriotism, he commenced his career by a breach of private confidence, and my correspondence, together with a letter of his own, containing nothing but false inferences, forced constructions, and gross and palpable falsehoods, were published in one of the Glasgow newspapers*.

The editor of the paper in which this correspondence was inserted, was, however, still more culpable for the erroneous impressions it produced. He had been personally acquainted with me for a considerable time, and knew most of my private as well as my public connexions; the columns of his paper had borne testimony to my principles and opinions on the state of public affairs, in being the first to direct attention to the sufferings of the labouring classes early in 1816; at which time I had predicted the very events that had taken place, and the measures which ought to have been adopted to prevent them. Admitting there were just grounds to entertain doubts of my integrity,

* Vide Glasgow Chronicle, 14th of August, 1817.

or the stability and sincerity of the principles I had professed, he was still without excuse. In the letters which he published, I directly mentioned the names of several gentlemen acquainted with all the circumstances, who had declared themselves perfectly satisfied with what I had done, as far as it affected the public interest; and the known and acknowledged character of the parties named, was a guarantee against them giving countenance to an invasion of individual right or public liberty. He had the means of ascertaining if that statement was correct, by a direct reference to some of the parties; and was, therefore, unjustifiable in not doing so, before he ventured to give publicity to the atrocious and unfounded calumnies of which he made his paper the vehicle. The evidence on the other side, which appeared to him sufficient to render all inquiry unnecessary, consisted in an admission, in my letters, that my efforts to dissipate the conspiracy were with the knowledge and sanction of government; together with a statement got up for M'Lachlan, in which that recreant contemptible apostate modestly affirmed, that he had no intention of attempting to form societies, to enforce universal sufferage and annual parliaments, until I suggested it to him, and pointed out the means of carrying it into effect. This miscreant was only the tool of a party, and the story got up was one mass of falsehood and misrepresentation, so incongruous and contradictory, that it could impose on no person of discernment, having a desire to arrive at the truth.

The temper of the times, however, admitted of no investigation; the olio of inconsistencies was unhesitatingly sworn to by the triple apostate, and, in the form of an affidavit, was inserted in the same paper with my letters; the sapient editor gravely assuring his readers, *that the whole state-*

ment must be held to be true, until each particular charge was distinctly disproven by direct evidence! Upon that authority, without farther inquiry, it was affirmed, that, through my agency, government was the author of the whole plot, and, the statement going the round of a certain portion of the periodical press, my name was immediately associated with a Reynolds, a Castles, and an Oliver. The editor of the paper in question asserted, that he was actuated by a sense of duty, but, without assuming the right of imputing motives, I may safely affirm, that the progress of rational liberty has been more impeded by the blunders of injudicious friends than the opposition of open enemies, and the purity of his intentions can only be defended at the expense of his judgment. If he aspired to the rank of becoming a benefactor to society, by exposing the malpractices of government, he ought to have availed himself of all the means his situation afforded, of arriving at the truth: this it was in his power to ascertain, and, if he failed in making use of the advantages he possessed, he was guilty of a gross dereliction of duty, which must have arisen from negligence, incapacity, or design. It was no abstract theoretical question, upon which a difference of opinion might exist, without any evil resulting from it, but a pure matter of fact, involving the most important consequences; and he ought to have been certain of the accuracy of every particular before he gave currency to statements, calculated to expose an individual to the execration of mankind, and still further widening the breach between the different ranks of society.

No permanent good can result from misrepresentations calculated to engender or foster antipathies between the government and the people; but it was more particularly reprehensible in a state of society, where the greatest evils have resulted from their knowing too little, and having no common feelings or sympathy with each other; and, at that particular period, government committed a sufficient number of errors, to render it unnecessary to augment or exaggerate its faults; chiefly, I believe, arising from ignorance of the actual condition of the people. Those who directly or indirectly encouraged the labouring population, while subjected to the severest privations and sufferings, to attempt to better their condition by violent means, and those who encouraged the government to have recourse to coercion, when justice and good policy required them to practise conciliation, were alike enemies to both; and of this I directly accuse the editor of the paper alluded to, as far as his influence extended. Whether his conduct proceeded from ignorance or design, it will not alter the case: the deep-rooted rancour produced by his representations, that government was the author of the conspiracy in 1817, was the direct cause and forerunner of those associations and tumultuous meetings which afterwards took place in the manufacturing districts of Scotland, and had their final consummation in bringing a few miserable, misguided men to the block, and the passing of the laws embodied in the memorable Six Acts, a part of which is to be transmitted down as a legacy to posterity. Like others who had laboured more extensively in the same vineyard, when the legitimate consequences of his conduct became apparent, he turned round and assailed the victims of his delusion, denying he had ever countenanced their opinions; but his pen was too feeble and impotent to stem the torrent he had contributed to raise, and the posthumous disavowal only illustrated his folly, want of foresight and ignorance of mankind.

After the publication of my letters, the columns of the same newspaper were daily thrown open to every species of personal abuse that could be levelled against me, to confirm the impression made. The object was to hunt me down, and, to an unconcerned spectator, it might have been amusing to observe the little mean arts had recourse to, to lower my character: the sanctuary of private life was openly violated; every assertion, however false, was related without examination into a single fact, and decided upon without the smallest attention to candour or justice. The productions were in themselves sufficiently puerile and contemptible; they were only conspicuous for a rancorous unmitigated malignity, that did little honour either to the writers or publishers; but they were adapted to the appetite of the multitude, nothing being too gross to be swallowed by popular credulity. Conscious of the falsity of the averments they had made, and believing that the refutation and exposure of the fraud practised on the public would chiefly depend upon my testimony, in anticipation of that exposure, all their ingenuity was exhausted in endeavours to shake the credit of any statement I might make. For this purpose the affidavit of M'Lachlan had been got up, that his spotless, untainted veracity might be pitted against mine; and, as they could find no instance in which I had previously violated any engagement in private or public life, they went a little out of their depth; but they astounded the multitude by soaring into the regions of abstract principles, and incontrovertibly established it as an axiom, that no statement of mine was entitled to credit, because I was a believer in the moral philosophy of Dr. Paley*.

* The editor of the paper being no adept in original composition, the libellous attacks appeared chiefly in the form of anonymous letters. Assuming the principle, that government had encouraged

My friends, who had previously entertained the strongest doubts of the public judging with candour or impartiality, and had therefore been most decidedly opposed to a public statement, now admitted the necessity of some step being taken to refute the calumnious allegations, as remarkable for their mendacity as the boldness with which they were made; and the only question for consideration was, the manner in which it could be done with the greatest propriety. The case was complicated and full of difficulties. On all sides the parties, although opposed to each other, had been

the getting up of the conspiracy, they endeavoured to produce an impression that I was without friends, and in a situation likely to be influenced by pecuniary considerations. They divested me of every good quality, leaving only the necessary portion of ability to carry the design into execution. Among the party, active and anxious to produce those impressions, were several who had abetted the conspiracy: they were the only persons above the labouring class who were in the secret, that had not been publicly implicated. By them the most virulent of the letters were written; and they affected profound ignorance of its existence until the parties were taken into custody. They believed they had escaped observation, and their design was obvious; but they were not aware that M'Lachlan, (and others,) the tool they were then making use of, had previously given information against them, and that it required every effort on my part, and the suppression of facts within my own knowledge, to prevent them being taken into custody. At the very time those attacks were publishing, it was a matter of deliberation whether, as a measure of precaution, they ought not to be secured under the Suspension Bill, which my representations successfully prevented. Had I been influenced by a similar spirit, how easily could I have retaliated, and how different has been the conduct manifested towards me. The editor could not be aware of all those facts, but, without inquiry, he inserted all the garbage presented to him; nor has the revolution of years, and a life spent aloof from all interference in public affairs, had any influence in preventing a petty and contemptible, but unrelenting and vindictive, persecution, that could proceed from nothing but a weak head or a bad heart. The filial duty of visiting the sick bed of one aged parent could not be performed, nor the last obsequies paid to the body of another, without his sacrilegious intrusion; and at the distance of four years, his pestiferous ribaldry continued to be spewed out, disturbing the last moments of the mother of my children.

guilty of errors, if not crimes, which they were studious to conceal, and in the midst of those opposing and contending interests I stood alone. Had I espoused the interest of one party, and concealed their errors, I might have had some chance of securing their suffrages in my favour; but by an open and candid development of the truth, I should have become the focus for the concentrated virulence of them all, and one common interest would have united them to throw discredit upon everything which depended upon my testimony. I would not, however, submit to any compromise or qualification, conceiving that the vindication of my character could only be effected, and the true interest of society promoted, by a complete exposure of the conduct of all the parties connected. It was no easy matter, however, to carry my views into execution; for, in addition to the party prejudice I had to encounter, another no less formidable difficulty presented itself. Pope, in one of his letters to Dr. Arbuthnot, says, "to attack vices in the abstract, without touching persons, may be safe fighting indeed, but it is fighting with shadows;" and my situation fully verified the truth of his remark. It would have served no purpose to point out errors without condescending upon the names of the individual actors, and the events were too green and the circumstances of the country peculiarly unfavourable for doing so, with a due regard either to the safety of individuals, or general utility. On account of those obstacles, my friends for some time hesitated between the propriety of a public statement and a judicial investigation, by an action against the paper that had published the libels; but, in the meantime, it was ascertained that it was intended to bring the case before parliament, which it was expected would afford me a safer opportunity, and more latitude for explanation. I had now nothing to dread so much as concealment or garbled partial disclosures, and I directed my whole attention to the point, for the double purpose of setting my own conduct in its proper point of view, and giving the country the benefit of every circumstance that had come to my knowledge. To effect this purpose, I left nothing undone that depended upon me; and as the circumstances attending it are rather singular, and tend to illustrate various traits of character in the different parties, I will give as concise an account of it as is consistent with a proper understanding of their conduct.

The ministry failed in establishing the guilt of all the persons they attempted to bring to trial in Yorkshire, as well as in the metropolis and in Scotland, but they made ample use of the powers vested in them by the Habeas Corpus Act Suspension Bill; and, during the whole of the summer of 1817, numbers of persons continued to be taken into custody, and were dispersed in different jails, at a distance from their usual places of residence. The operation of that law, or rather the total absence of all law, placed the liberty of every person, liable to suspicion, at the mercy of any mercenary, unprincipled informer; and, whether they might be justly or unjustly accused, the country had no means of ascertaining. A power so extensive, and even in the best hands so liable to abuse, must, in a country having any pretensions to liberty, always excite a strong degree of jealousy; and the absence of all legal proof of the treasonable practices of the persons accused made a very strong feeling prevail, that those powers had been exercised with undue severity; nor was the opinion very generally entertained of the personal character of the Noble

Lord at the head of the Home Department, at all calculated to allay that feeling. The convictions which took place at Derby, towards the end of October, were attended with so many suspicious circûmstances, that it rather increased than diminished the desire for inquiry; and, for some time previous to the opening of the session of 1818, the most active members in opposition to the ministry were busily engaged in collecting such information as would enable them to expose the errors of their internal policy. The result of those inquiries was, a determination to bring forward specific charges for separate acts of misgovernment and abuse of power, which were comprised under three distinct heads: viz. Oppressions committed under the powers conferred by the Suspension Bill. 2d, The alleged attempt of the crown lawyers of Scotland to suborn evidence. And 3d, The employment of spies, who, it was asserted, had acted as incendiaries. It was at first intended to bring a formal charge of that nature against me. Lord Archibald Hamilton had interested himself in inquiring into the circumstances connected with the conspiracy at Glasgow, and, deceived by the specious representations of the party who had attacked me, he pledged himself to bring forward a charge against me in the House of Commons. On learning that determination, I indulged a hope that it would lead to a full investigation; but I felt anxious, if it was brought forward at all, that the minutest inquiry should take place. From all I could learn of the character and conduct of the persons employed by the government in England, their proceedings, if not absolutely criminal, afforded strong ground of suspicion; and I did not wish my character and conduct to be mixed up and confounded with that of a set of men who, (even admitting their services had been useful, in a political point of view,) there was every reason to believe, had been actuated by very different motives, and were entitled to no merit, as moral agents. I therefore resolved to take every precaution not to allow it to evaporate in vague and general discussion, which could only tend to make the matter worse. My situation was, however, in the highest degree delicate and embarrassing, as none of the parties, interested on my account, could communicate with each other. The Lord Advocate and Mr. Finlay were the only persons who had seats in the House, that were acquainted with all the circumstances. Both of them *professed* a strong desire that justice should be done to my character, but they could take no measures in common, for, from the time the latter had charged the former gentleman with incapacity, all intercourse between them had ceased. Mr. Jeffrey and Mr. Cockburn interested themselves warmly in the matter, but their opinions were too much at variance with the general policy pursued, to admit of their communicating with any of the members of government.

It was my first object to ascertain if the ministry would sanction an inquiry, and I pointed out to the Lord Advocate the advantages which would be derived from following that course. I told him that a deep impression had been made upon the minds of the mass of the people, that government had acted unfairly toward them; that, if errors had been committed, it would have a much better effect to acknowledge them candidly; and, on the contrary, if they were convinced they had acted properly, nothing could be so pernicious as throwing a veil of intrigue and mystery over matters which ought to have been prosecuted boldly and as openly avowed; that I was most anxious to avow and explain everything I had done and every circumstance that had come under my observation, and I urged him to press the propriety of having me examined at the bar of the House of Commons, or by a committee, if one was appointed. Whether my representations made any impression, or whether they ever had hesitated about the propriety of sanctioning an inquiry, I am unable to say, but it was some time before the Lord Advocate could inform me what course they intended to pursue, until it drew near the opening of the session, when he told me it was determined to resist every attempt at inquiry whatever. The reason he assigned was, that it would be a violation of every principle of state policy, to permit inquiry into the internal measures of government; that, as far as I had been concerned, he was satisfied it would be attended with advantage; but he had reason to know *matters had been very differently conducted in several parts of England,* and, were the general principle admitted, inquiry could not be conceded in one point without conceding it in all, so that the only alternative was, to resist it altogether; that the opposition in parliament were equally aware that the principle could never be admitted, and that they were only making a pretext for the purpose of embarrassing the government; but if they attempted to arraign my conduct in the house, he would be ready in his place to defend it.

Conscious that the ministry could easily command a majority to quash all regular inquiry, this declaration put an end to any hope I had entertained of having an opportunity of explaining my own case. I was also aware that, if an attack was made upon me, and my defence was left to the Lord Advocate, or any member of administration, it would be considered, by three-fourths of the community, as tantamount to a sentence of condemnation. I therefore applied to Mr. Jeffrey, to endeavour to procure some independent member, of weight and influence, or, at all events, some of the members connected with the opposition, to bring forward my case, and he immediately informed several; amongst whom were Mr. Abercrombie, Mr. Brougham, and Mr. Grant, of Rothiemurchus. Mr. Brougham made the most minute inquiries of Mr. Jeffrey, as to his knowledge of my previous character, as well as into all the circumstances connected with that particular transaction; and I waited for a considerable time to learn the determination. Nothing, however, transpired until a few days before the opening of the session, when Mr. Jeffrey informed me that, at a meeting of the members connected with the opposition, held in the house of Earl Grey, for the purpose of arranging the plan of the parliamentary campaign, my case had been fully considered. That they were satisfied I had been influenced by laudable motives, and that there appeared to be nothing reprehensible in my conduct; but, if *they* brought the matter forward in the house, for the purpose of vindicating me, the ministry would immediately take advantage of it, as a set-off against the case of Oliver and others, which admitted of no such justification. It had, therefore, been resolved to avoid introducing it altogether, and to confine the charge to the crown lawyers and others, in official situations, for subornation of evidence.

Thus were all my endeavours, and the hopes I had entertained of having the matter fully explained in parliament, frustrated; and it exhibits a practical lesson of the *justice* resulting from the collision of parties, which requires no comment. It was, however, exactly what Mr. Jeffrey had foretold, although he made every exertion in his power to prevent it. Baffled in all those attempts, one resource only remained, which was, to endeavour to induce Mr. Finlay to bring it forward in the house; and, for this purpose, I went to Glasgow, and had a personal interview with him previous to his going to London. He was, above all other persons, more immediately bound to see justice done to me, and best qualified to enter into the necessary explanations. Whether he was afraid of exposing his own conduct by explaining mine, I will not pretend to say, my readers must form their own judgment, by a reference to the preceding details; but I found him altogether averse to agitating the subject in parliament, although he faithfully promised to enter fully into the question, if brought up by any other member in the course of the expected discussions.

Under those circumstances the session of parliament opened, and, in a few days, Lord Archibald Hamilton preferred the charges against the crown lawyers of Scotland. The only evidence which could be adduced to prove their delinquency was the deposition of Campbell, as given on the trial, which was met by a decided negative by the Lord Advocate, in name of all the parties accused. It was therefore the veracity of one party opposed to the veracity of another; and, if the collective body of the House of Commons is to be considered a correct judge of what constitutes the test of truth, the crown lawyers were in the right, for the question was decided in their favour by a large majority*.

* The opposition were so extremely cautious and secret in arranging their plans, previous to the opening of the session, that the crown lawyers in vain endeavoured to discover the points they were to be attacked upon. In consequence of the breach with Mr. Finlay, the Lord Advocate depended entirely upon me for a detail of all the facts which had not occurred within his own

In the discussion on Scotch affairs, no allusion whatever was made to my case, which excited no little surprise in the minds of my *good friends* in Glasgow, who were altogether ignorant of the cause; and believing there were no means of con-

knowledge, to enable him to refute or palliate whatever charges might be preferred against him. Each of the parties knew that I was communicating with the others; but my situation was extremely embarrassing, as I became the depositary of what each, for the time being, wished to keep secret. With a just feeling for the delicacy of my situation, Mr. Jeffrey, as much as possible, refrained from introducing any topic not directly connected with my own case; but he could not avoid mentioning the points to which the attack was to be confined, in the understanding that I was not to put the crown lawyers on their guard against it. The Lord Advocate expected to obtain the information he required, on his arrival in London. In this he was, however, disappointed; nor did the manner in which Lord Archibald Hamilton gave notice of his motion throw any light upon the subject; and, in this dilemma, he wrote express to the Solicitor General, to urge me to obtain the information from some of my friends. When the Solicitor General applied to me, I told him he was aware I had never broken confidence with them; and that, in the most trying circumstances, I had refrained from all communication with my friends until the last moment, to which I had given my pledge, had expired, and that he could not expect me to act upon a different principle with others; that I knew distinctly upon what points the charges were to be preferred, but it had been communicated to me in confidence, for my personal satisfaction, and I did not consider myself at liberty to give any information respecting it. The Solicitor General replied, that my conduct was candid and honourable in that instance, as well as it had been in others; that he had not another word to say, as they were entitled to meet the charges against them in the best manner they could, without subjecting me to further inquiry. My feeble testimony can add little to the character of that gentleman; but I owe it in justice to his memory to say, that, in all my intercourse with him, which included many an hour's general conversation, his conduct was in the highest degree candid and honourable. With no showy or very brilliant talents, he had a high-toned aristocratic feeling, which induced him to consider the *plebeian order* of too little consequence in society; but he disdained to stoop to anything mean to accomplish an object, and had too much straight-forward honesty to evince any of the Machiavelian suppleness of the statesman. He frankly admitted many of the errors committed by government; one of which was, that, as far as it respected Scotland, there was no necessity for the Suspension Bill in 1817.

troverting their misrepresentations, they again urged Lord Archibald Hamilton to bring it forward. That noble Lord attempted to redeem his pledge at a subsequent period, at the close of a debate on a motion made by Mr. Fazakerley, to inquire into the conduct of Oliver; but as soon as he introduced my name, he was immediately beat down by the uproar and noise from the opposition benches. Trivial as was this circumstance, it afforded Mr. Finlay a fair opportunity for entering into explanation, had he felt any serious inclination to do so; and the only apology he attempted to make, in answer to my repeated remonstrances, for allowing that opportunity to slip, was, that the little that had been said required no answer, nobody having attended to it, and the house would hear nothing farther on the subject.

In the numerous discussions which took place in parliament, relative to the internal policy of government, during the sessions of 1818-19, my name was never again mentioned; but whatever evil resulted to society, from the conduct of the different parties, no blame can be attachable to me, as I did every thing in my power to bring the case forward in the only places where it could have been properly discussed. I was made the victim of their contending interests; for, when men of the first rank and education, to serve a party purpose, suffered me to remain under imputations, calculated to drive a person of well-regulated mind almost beyond the pale of civilized society, greater impartiality was not to be expected from others less favourably situated; while a public appeal would have been equally ineffectual, amidst the ferments consequent on the measures then pursued. My friends, indeed, were united in opinion that, under existing circumstances, no effort I could make would remove the impression; and, as my private prospects were irretrievably ruined, there was no other resource but to press the government for indemnification, and, writhing under all the tortures of mental agony, the situation of my family obliged me to submit to the humiliating alternative.

From that period, my intercourse with the parties with whom I had become involved being confined entirely to personal concerns, minute detail will be deemed superfluous by those who consider nothing interesting which has not a direct relation to public events. The task I have imposed upon myself is not a very gracious one; and where the narrator can derive no pleasure or gratification himself, and is in doubt of being able to communicate instruction or amusement to others, brevity must always be most desirable. The remaining part of my personal narrative can develop no new principle or spring of action. Circumstances of a similar kind have a thousand times occurred, and have been as often reiterated. It can, therefore, only be interesting, in as far as it may point out individuals to have been possessed of the good or bad qualities which belong to our common nature. In a moral point of view, it is admitted to be as necessary to the wellbeing of society, to expose the weakness, errors, and vices of those placed in conspicuous situations, as to point out examples of a contrary tendency; but the latter will always be more gratifying to a well-regulated mind, while the former must always appear rather invidious, and attended with some degree of suspicion, when accompanied by the idea of real or supposed personal injustice. To that charge I may be exposed, but a relation of facts, in such a case, is the best commentary. My object is, to show men as they are, not as they ought to be; and if that relation should exhibit indecision, bad faith, pitiful shuffling, and tergiversation unworthy of men filling high official situations, my own character is equally open to examination.

At the interview Mr. Finlay had with Lord Sidmouth, relative to my situation, at the close of the session of 1817, already alluded to, it was agreed that the Lord Advocate, as official organ, should conduct the arrangement, to whom Lord Sidmouth engaged to communicate his sentiments, Mr. Finlay not being to interfere, unless the Lord Advocate failed to arrange it satisfactorily. It was almost immediately after ascertained, that the case was to become the subject of parliamentary discussion, in consequence of which nothing whatever was done; it being agreed, upon all hands, it would be better to allow it to stand over until the result of the discussions was known. The Lord Advocate returned to Scotland, in high spirits, immediately after the disposal of Lord Archibald Hamilton's motion, in February, 1818, when he told me, [I quote his Lordship's express words,] "that all parties in parliament were satisfied I had done my duty to society in a correct and honourable manner; as a proof of which, none of the other side of the house dared even to whisper my name, although well acquainted with all the particulars; that he had explained my conduct and situation at the Treasury Board, after the debate was over in the house, where it had been fully discussed; that they were all sensible I had had a very difficult task to perform, and must have suffered much; but that I had conducted myself so entirely to the satisfaction of all who were acquainted with the true state of affairs, that he was determined—the first minister of the country was determined—nay, the whole Treasury Board were determined—that I should be fully compensated, and that I should be placed in a situation which would enable me to live comfortably during the remainder of my life." He added, that some delay would take place before the arrangement could be completed, as they wished the thing to be entirely blown over, and they were also hurried with the approaching elections; but, in the mean time, I was to allow myself to suffer no pecuniary inconvenience, as he would give me a draft upon his banker for any money I required.

I depicted, in the most vivid colours, the misery I suffered by being kept so long in a state of suspense, and urged his Lordship to press the matter to as speedy a decision as possible; but nothing definite took place until the 26th of May, when he informed me, that the ministry were afraid they would be *drawn over the coals* by the opposition, if they made any appointment directly under their own patronage*. He was, therefore, requested to submit it, for my consideration, to accept an outfit to the Cape of Good Hope, where I should receive a grant of land, accompanied with a strong recommendation to the governor of the colony. My answer to this important proposition was requested in two days, which afforded little time to consult my friends. The same reasons, however, which prevented me from accepting the

* Their fears arose from the attacks made against them at that period, in parliament, for appointing Mr. Reynolds to a Consulship. That person had been deeply implicated in the confederacy which led to the rebellion in Ireland, in 1798; and, after making discoveries to government, became the leading witness for the crown, on the trials of M'Cann, Byrne, and Bond, his former associates, who were all convicted of high treason. He afterwards became the special protegée of the late Marquis of Londonderry, then Secretary of State for Ireland; and his former conduct was resuscitated, by his being most injudiciously and improperly appointed one of the jury for the County of Middlesex, on the trials for treason, in 1817.

offer made by them, to go to America, operated in a still stronger degree here, when the vague and indefinite principle upon which I should have to go out, and the circumstances of the colony were fully taken into consideration. At the time appointed, therefore, I waited upon the Lord Advocate and stated my reasons for rejecting the offer.

On this occasion a rather singular conversation took place. After fully explaining to him, that I could not go to a distant foreign station, without exposing my family to the greatest hazard and doing the utmost violence to my own feelings, I told him, that the objection stated against making an arrangement at home appeared to me to be completely puerile, and, in point of fact, was no objection at all, as the case did not apply; that I claimed no *reward* for the services which it was acknowledged I had rendered, but indemnification for the positive loss I had sustained; that no pecuniary compensation they could give, could ever atone for the mental sufferings I had undergone; but that the prejudice which had been excited against me, had deprived me of all equal chance in society, and that I considered them in honour bound to make up my losses, to such an extent at least as to enable me to maintain a rank in society equal to the one I could have held by my own exertion, and I wanted no more; that the leading members of the opposition in parliament were perfectly sensible how the matter stood, and that it was no parallel case to those they had objected to; that I most ardently desired *they* would bring it forward, to give me an opportunity of entering into such explanations as would remove a part of the prejudice existing out of doors; but, by the principle upon which both parties had acted, they denied me that privilege, and I would not, unless I were compelled, expatriate myself, until I had the means of explaining with some hope of success. He then replied, that they did not attach much importance to any attempt of the opposition to impugn their conduct; but the chief difficulty which prevented government from making an appointment to a situation directly under their patronage, arose from their fear of being *overwhelmed* with solicitations in behalf of men who had been employed in England, for whom they neither had, nor were disposed to make, any provision; that, although government were perfectly sensible of the difference between my case and theirs, they did not wish to be forced to enter into explanations to the applicants on the behalf of those men, which such an appointment would render unavoidable; but that he would inform Lord Sidmouth of the nature of my objections to the propositions submitted, and let me know the import of his answer as soon as he received it. The session of parliament terminated, however, without any communication being made to me, although the Bill of Indemnity had *justified* ministers for all their proceedings, which was considered to put an end to farther discussion; and when I importuned the Lord Advocate, he told me he had written repeatedly without obtaining any definite answer. As he could take no responsibility upon himself, at his request, I drew up a short representation of all the facts and circumstances, which he forwarded to Lord Sidmouth, on the 2d of September; but it had no better success.

Mr. Reddie had, from the commencement, felt an intense interest in my situation, and as I kept up a regular correspondence with him, he remonstrated strongly against the injustice of keeping me so long in suspense; to which the Lord Advocate answered, he was not at all blameable, as he had pressed the matter until, he believed, he had rendered himself disagreeable. As all parties had been alike liberal in their professions, it was difficult for me to judge whose conduct was really censurable. My friends, however, were agreed in opinion, that I had completely exhausted the official quarter in Scotland, and I told the Lord Advocate that, as I looked upon Mr. Finlay in honour bound to see justice done to me, I would immediately call upon him to interfere. At a former period his Lordship had told me the matter had been intrusted entirely to himself, and that he felt sufficiently interested, on my account, to render Mr. Finlay's interference unnecessary; but he now assured me, if Mr. Finlay, or any other person, could be of service, in supporting his representations, he was perfectly agreeable they should do so. Mr. Finlay had been some time absent, in France, but, previous to his leaving England, it had been agreed, if any obstacle was thrown in the way of a settlement, he should be instantly apprised of it; and, early in October, Mr. Reddie forwarded to him copies of my correspondence with the Lord Advocate, and, as soon as he arrived in London, he solicited an interview with Lord Sidmouth. A meeting took place, in consequence, on the 17th of the above month, after which Mr. Finlay wrote me, that the representation had been transmitted by the Lord Advocate and fully considered; that my services and motives were as warmly and justly appreciated by all the parties as they were by himself, and as strong a desire existed to do me justice, but that difficulties were in the way of accomplishing that desire, which he would be better able to explain at a future period; that, in the mean time, an annuity should be paid me, to meet my running expenses, on a moderate scale, until a more permanent arrangement should be made.

When the proposal was made for me to go to the Cape of Good Hope, Mr. Finlay gave it as his opinion that, whatever engagement I entered into, I ought to have it committed to writing, *as their verbal promises were not worth a straw.* He, however, now stated, he had the most perfect reliance on the promise made to him being faithfully performed, although I was never able to learn the ground upon which he had changed his opinion; nor did I receive any explanation of the causes which prevented a determinate settlement. He desired me to make no allusion to the arrangement he had concluded, in any of my communications with the Lord Advocate, as it would be officially announced to him, in the usual way, with authority to affix the times and manner of paying the annuity. When I called on the Lord Advocate, he denied having received intimation of any settlement whatever; and, after various applications, told me, on the 11th of January, 1819, that he had, in repeated letters, pressed my claims in the most urgent manner; that he had represented it as a case in which he was personally interested, and for which he considered himself personally responsible, but he had never obtained any satisfactory answer, either as to the cause of the delay or the time it would exist. That the money he had advanced was out of his *own means;* which he had considered himself bound to do, both from a sense of duty and personal feeling, even if it should never be refunded, of which he was very uncertain. That he had been apprised of Mr. Finlay having called at Lord Sidmouth's office, and was glad he had done so, as by that means I might learn he was dealing fairly with me; for he saw no possible reason for their acting as they were doing. That it was a case of most excessive hardship, but he would endeavour to come to an understanding on the matter, when he went up to attend his duty in parliament. I told his Lordship that, however much I felt obliged for his humanity, I had no wish to lay myself under any personal obligation, as I considered, upon every principle of honour and justice, my claim was one of right, and not of grace or favour.

I apprised Mr. Reddie, from time to time, of the difficulties thrown in the way, even of the temporary measure which Mr. Finlay had represented as concluded; and early in February, my letters, detailing all that had transpired with the Lord Advocate, were forwarded to Mr. Finlay in London. On the 8th of that month, he again waited upon Lord Sidmouth, and, by a letter of that day's date, I was informed, that he had received assurances that immediate instructions should be given to pay up the arrears of the annuity which had been promised, and to continue it by regular instalments, until a satisfactory arrangement could be made; that the Lord Advocate had called the same day, and had urged the matter very strongly; and that I might rest myself quite easy, for my desire to have the whole matter settled could hardly be stronger than it was there. About three weeks after, the Lord Advocate was called down to Scotland for a short time on business, when I waited upon him, never entertaining a doubt but he was fully authorized to make a formal recognition of the engagement made with Mr. Finlay. He, however, denied all knowledge of any specific arrangement; saying, that no settlement could be got at the time, but that *he understood* there were some arrears due, to enable me to meet present exigencies, the particulars of which he would explain before he left Scotland. That explanation was, however, never given, as he went off a few days after, leaving notice that he could give no satisfaction until he returned to London, when he would write to me immediately on his arrival; and, in a short time after, he sent me an order for some money, without making a single allusion to the principle upon which the remittance was made. At this time I met with a severe domestic affliction in the death of my only son; and harassed and worn out with such tantalizing treatment, I was for some time incapable of prosecuting the matter further.

Things, therefore, remained in the above situation until the middle of June, when the sudden and unexpected death of Lord Reston, one of the judges of the Court of Session, produced a change in the law arrangements in Scotland. The Lord Advocate was raised to the bench, under the title of Lord Meadowbank, and Sir William Rae, the present Lord Advocate, appointed to succeed him in office. Lord Meadowbank arrived in Edinburgh on the 21st of June; and, soon after, I wrote him a letter, representing that the gentleman who was to succeed him in office having no knowledge of me, nor of the circumstances, could not be expected to feel an equal degree of interest in the case; that, from the interest he had professed to feel, *and the personal obligation which he considered himself under*, to see justice done, I expected he would bring it to a definite conclusion before resigning it into the hands of his successor. On no notice being taken of this letter, nor another of a similar import, which I sent some time after, Mr. Reddie remonstrated with him on the impropriety of not coming to an explicit understanding with his successor, to prevent the necessity of disagreeable repetitions; and, on the 27th of July, he acquainted Mr. Reddie, that he had settled everything in a satisfactory manner before he resigned his former office. Mr. Reddie accompanied this intelligence with a request, that I should call personally upon his Lordship; and, on the 4th of August, I waited upon him, when he shortly informed me that he declined all farther interference, having left it to the Secretary of State and Sir William Rae; that he had explained everything to the latter gentleman, and would send me a card of introduction to him in the course of the evening. I received an open card a few days afterwards, which was, verbatim, as follows:—"The bearer is Mr. Richmond, the circumstances of whose case I fully explained to your Lordship." When I waited upon Sir William Rae with this note, he told me that *he had not seen Lord Meadowbank, nor did he know any thing of the case;* but that he would write to the Secretary of State for instructions how to act, and inform me of the result*.

The session of Parliament being closed, Mr. Finlay was then in Scotland, and he and Mr. Reddie expressed the greatest indignation, when I informed them of Lord Meadowbank's conduct, and that he had made no arrangement whatever with

* This finished my correspondence with Lord Meadowbank, and the detail conveys no very prepossessing view of his character or conduct. How far he might have been controlled by others, it is impossible for me to judge. In some instances, where I solicited small favours for others, in matters immediately under his own control, I found him ready to oblige, and prompt in execution, and he treated me always with the greatest affability and respect. It was rumoured in the law circle, at the time, that he was himself disappointed; that he considered his services entitled him to the situation of Lord Chief Baron in the Court of Exchequer, which office was then about to become vacant; but the superior services or interest of Sir Samuel Shepherd, the English Attorney General, superseded him. Admitting, however, that he felt chagrined at the ministry for *underrating* his services, it will be difficult to reconcile his professions with his conduct in my case; and, supposing he had been guilty of no previous neglect, his ceasing to take any interest on my account, the moment he found he was to change his official situation, is not easily reconcileable either with justice or correct feeling.

his successor. Mr. Finlay immediately wrote to Lord Sidmouth, remonstrating against the non-fulfilment of the promise made to him; and Sir William Rae, having occasion to be on business at Glasgow, Mr. Reddie and Mr. Finlay had an opportunity of partially introducing the subject to him personally. A few days afterwards he wrote me to call upon him, which I did, on the 31st of August, when he stated, that he was ignorant of particulars, but understood I had been very badly used, and that it was his decided opinion that not a moment's delay ought to have taken place in settling a matter of the kind; that he did not consider it necessary that he should be made acquainted with the particulars, as government were fully aware of them, and he was not likely to have any control over them. He then produced two letters he had received from Lord Sidmouth; the first directing him to pay the annuity they had promised, upwards of six months of it being then due; and the second, which was of a subsequent date, requesting him to furnish me with copies of the circular letter issued from the Colonial Office, respecting emigration to Algoa Bay, at the Cape of Good Hope. I was requested to weigh the matter maturely, and if I would agree to go out, he was desired to assure me I would receive an outfit, and a strong recommendation to the civil government; in other words, it was a repetition of the offer made the preceding year, which I had then declined; but whether it was considered that time, and the schooling I had received, had enlightened my judgment and qualified me better for the situation of an African backwoodsman, must be left for those to determinate who renewed the proposition. The Lord Advocate declining all interference, requested me to return him a written answer, to be transmitted to Lord Sidmouth; and, although nothing had occurred to induce me to change my sentiments, I did not wish to do any thing hastily or unadvisedly, and I again submitted the matter to my friends. I went to Glasgow and had a meeting with Messrs. Finlay and Reddie, when the whole of my treatment was fully discussed. I pointed out difficulties which appeared to me insurmountable, and they and my friends coincided entirely in my opinion; for, besides the objections of a general nature, (already mentioned,) against leaving the country, there were others of a particular description, applying to the settlement at the Cape, which the fate of the unfortunate Colonists at Algoa Bay has since but too fatally realized. It was therefore agreed that I should finally reject the offer; and, on the 21st of September, I returned an answer to the Lord Advocate, detailing my reasons at length, which he immediately transmitted to London.

On the 6th of October I had a card from his Lordship, requesting to see me. He informed me he had received an answer from the Secretary of State, importing, that as I declined going to the Cape on the terms proposed, government preferred settling my claim in money. That he was directed to inquire what sum I would consider a fair indemnification, he being, to a certain extent, empowered to settle it, if we could agree upon the amount. I told him I had no objection to the principle of such an arrangement, but felt a delicacy in condescending upon any specific sum; and, as he had no knowledge of the circumstances, it was impossible for him to form an adequate idea of the case. I therefore proposed to refer it to Messrs. Finlay and Reddie, as the most competent judges; and that I would submit to any decision they thought proper to give. To this proposition he, however, objected. He said, that government did not wish a reference to be made to any third party, and he was instructed to ascertain my own opinion, which he wished to have in a day or two at farthest. When I called upon him again, I repeated my objection to mention any sum, and that there was no necessity for any delicacy with Mr. Finlay or Mr. Reddie, who, in all the previous stages, had communicated directly with the Home Secretary and the late Lord Advocate; and I again insisted for reference being made to them. He, however, persisted in having my own opinion first; and when I partially explained the positive loss I had sustained, by the total ruin of all my prospects, viewed only in a pecuniary light, and apart from the injury done to my feelings, he said it involved a question of much greater magnitude than he had been led to believe; that it was impossible for him to be a proper judge, and, although it had been in some measure left to his discretion, he knew that government did not expect him to go to the extent which, from the view I had given, such a case would require. That he did not wish to take any side in the question, but would transmit any representation which I chose to make; and, as he was of opinion it had been too long delayed, that I should also write Mr. Finlay, and get it brought to a conclusion at once.

After fully ascertaining Messrs. Finlay and Reddie's opinions, and consulting with my friends, on the 28th of October, I gave in a representation, explaining the nature of my situation and expectations in 1816, when Mr. Finlay solicited my interference, with all the consequences that had followed, in a manner which might enable the Secretary of State clearly to comprehend the principle upon which the value of a sum of money was to be estimated, in the circumstances in which it had placed me; and concluded by alluding to the solemn assurance given at a former period, that the injuries I had sustained would be repaired, as far as it could be effected by pecuniary compensation.

Having learnt that the Lord Advocate had received an answer to the above communication, I called upon him on the 13th of November, when he read me an extract of a letter from Mr. Hobhouse, to the following effect:—"That he had laid his Lordship's letter, with the enclosure, before Lord Sidmouth, and was directed by him to say, with respect to the claims of Richmond, they appear to be *greatly inflated; government never having given him any assurance that they would place him in a situation where he would live comfortable during the remainder of his life*; that Lord Sidmouth adhered to the instructions formerly given," which was, to offer a sum, not amounting to one-fourth of my actual loss, "and, whether I accepted it or not, the Lord Advocate was directed to discontinue the annuity previously granted." The Lord Advocate added, that I certainly must have been deceived or mistaken; for he believed Lord Sidmouth was a *very honest man*, and would not deny any promise he had made, or refuse to redeem any pledge he had given. I replied that, as his Lordship knew nothing of the particulars, it was of little use for me to expostulate with him, but that my feelings had been outraged and trifled with, in a most wanton and cruel manner; that, whether promises had been made or not, did not alter the nature of right, and I only wished to have what I was in justice entitled to, as I made no claim upon their generosity; that when the prejudice I had to encounter, from those who had no knowledge of my conduct and previous situation, was taken into consideration, I had a right to expect other treatment from those who did; and, although I could not conceive a question of right at all depended upon the faith of promises, it remained to be shown whether Lord Sidmouth or others had asserted a falsehood, for I had a sufficient number of written documents in my possession to prove the accuracy of my statement*. I added, that as his Lordship's predecessor and others had thought proper to act in the manner they had done, I had only Messrs. Finlay and Reddie to look to; and, as I must decline his Lordship's offer, I would immediately acquaint them with the circumstances.

The same day on which Messrs. Finlay and Reddie received my letter, conveying the above intelligence, they had an opportunity of meeting the Lord Advocate in Glasgow; when Mr. Finlay told him, in a very decided manner, that he considered the obligation sacred, on the part of government, to pay the annuity they had promised, until they made some other arrangement more satisfactory to me. After hearing Messrs. Finlay and Reddie's opinion, it was agreed, that he should be furnished with a memorandum of the services I had rendered, and that he and Mr. Finlay should, together, wait upon Lord Sidmouth, on their arrival in London, at the opening of the session, which was to take place in a few days. Some delay took place, after their arrival in London, in consequence of a more special statement being required from Mr. Reddie, before a conference could take place. They did

* His Lordship seemed rather surprised at this information; imagining, I presume, that all the parties ought to have acted with the same official caution as himself, he having carefully abstained from attaching his signature to any of the notes he had sent me; and, on hearing it, observed, that I had better think over the matter for a few days.

not, however, see Lord Sidmouth, but the representation was presented to Mr. Hobhouse, by the Lord Advocate and Mr. Finlay, about the middle of December, accompanied with a strong recommendation and opinion, that the sum proposed as an indemnification was altogether inadequate. I did not learn the result of the representation, until the 4th of January, 1820, when the Lord Advocate, who was in Scotland during the Christmas recess, sent me a note to call upon him; when he read me a letter he had received from Mr. Hobhouse, to the following effect: "That he had laid the written statement, put into his hands, before Lord Sidmouth, and related the substance of the conversation which he had the honour to have with his Lordship and Mr. Finlay, relative to A. Richmond; and he was directed by his Lordship to say, that, without throwing any reflection on the manner he came to be involved, the circumstances mentioned were not known to his Majesty's Government, until a considerable time after they had occurred; Lord Sidmouth, therefore, cannot agree to allow more than the sum already specified." I told the Lord Advocate that, as he disavowed being a party, and had apparently done everything in his power, I would make no remark upon the original merits of the case; but, supposing the objection stated to be true, it was no reason why they should act unjustly, when the circumstances came to their knowledge; that, in point of fact, I had been led to believe it was altogether different, and I must therefore have recourse to those who had repeatedly assured me that government had solemnly pledged themselves to see me fully indemnified.

Against this decision of the Home Secretary Mr. Reddie again strongly remonstrated, and Mr. Finlay, by a letter of the 20th of January, informed me that, on learning the import of the answer to the former representation, he had waited on Lord Sidmouth the preceding day, and had stated his opinion in so decided a manner, that the matter was in a fair way of being adjusted, by my being appointed to a place as originally stipulated. Notwithstanding all I could urge, however, I could obtain no information of the nature or locality of the situation proposed, to enable me to make any domestic arrangement until the 11th of April; when Mr. Reddie wrote me, they had at last received a *written assurance* from the *proper authority*, that the promises made to me by the late Lord Advocate would be in every respect fulfilled; and that, in the mean time, the annuity should be continued, no part of it having been paid from August 1819*. No specific measure, how-

* I give the circumstances which produced this assurance, as a specimen of the intrinsic value of the promises of the late Right Honourable Secretary. In the earlier stages of the business, although he had been very profuse in his professions to give me a liberal indemnification, they were all verbal, and sufficiently vague and general to enable him to give his own definition of the term. When Mr. Finlay called upon him, in January, and told him what he considered my former prospects and conduct entitled me to, and the assurances that had been given me by the late Lord Advocate in his Lordship's name, he sheltered himself under cover of the Lord Advocate having exceeded his powers, if he had given any such assurance as I had represented.

When Mr. Finlay applied for my assistance, in December 1816, he had received two letters from the Lord Advocate, authorising him to offer me a situation under government, of a certain specified value, as an inducement for me to lend my assistance. The precise amount of the value of the situation offered I never knew; for, as I formerly mentioned, I at once peremptorily spurned the idea of acting from such a motive. Mr. Finlay had, however, preserved the two letters, and to bring the matter to a point, he had recourse to them on that occasion. Lord Sidmouth expressed a wish to see the documents, not seeming to depend altogether upon his word, but Mr. Finlay could not, at the time, produce them, he having them deposited in his private bureau in Glasgow, and could not procure them until he was there personally. On the adjourning of parliament, in consequence of

ever, resulted from this notification, except that the annuity was very partially paid up.

I had now no direct communication with the Lord Advocate, nor could I ascertain anything but through the medium of Mr. Finlay; and although, in letter after letter, I pointed out in the most forcible light the sufferings my family endured from being kept in suspense, he became so exceedingly reserved in his communications, that I could obtain nothing but evasive answers; until, by a letter dated the 18th of June, I was informed he had had a conversation relative to my business; that he found the difficulties in the way of a permament settlement fully as great as ever, and, if there were any difference, even greater; that the annuity would be regularly continued, through his medium, until the situation promised was procured, but I could obtain no assurance when it would take place; it might occur in the course of a week, or it might not take place for years, unless the whole matter was terminated by an agreement to pay a specific sum of money, in full of all demands.

This was the last personal conference held at the Home Department. Mr. Finlay at this period retiring from parliament, all future correspondence was carried on by letter. The matter was now conducted entirely by Messrs. Finlay and Reddie, the Lord Advocate, disgusted with such vacillating conduct, having refused all further interference; and, unable to obtain any kind of

the death of the late King, he went down to Scotland about the end of February, when he sent the documents to the Home Secretary, Mr. Reddie accompanying them with a letter urging my claims, and stating that, whether the late Lord Advocate had exceeded his powers or not, the first law officer of the crown in Scotland was at a very low ebb indeed, if he could not, in a case of emergency, guarantee a paltry situation. This produced the answer above stated, when Mr. Finlay returned to London in April.

security which would enable me to put my family in any settled situation, I wrote them, that as the basis of an accommodation was laid by the principle of indemnification by a sum of money, being recognised by both parties, the only difference which could arise must be respecting the amount; that as there was no appearance of obtaining a settlement upon other terms, I put it entirely into their hands; that they were perfectly aware of the difficulties I had to encounter, and the sufferings I had been exposed to, but that they were to sacrifice everything which might have been considered due to my feelings, as they had to deal with men who seemed incapable of appreciating them, as my friends had foretold; and, as the question would be thereby reduced to the actual loss I had sustained, I would accept of any sum which they might consider reasonable.

The negociation was accordingly renewed upon that basis, and continued until the end of September, when Mr. Reddie apprised me that, after making every effort in their power, they were unable to induce government to give anything at all like a reasonable indemnification, even on the principle laid down; and that, after comparing it with the disadvantages attendant on remaining in a state of insecurity and uncertainty, I might draw my own conclusion. Mr. Finlay had, for a considerable time, exhibited more of the cold caution of the politician than the interest or warmth of a friend. My annuity was never paid up, according to agreement. It seemed to have been the object to tire me out, as well as every one who felt an interest on my account, by interminable delay, and it was thoroughly accomplished. The patience of all was exhausted, nor did any hope remain, that the moral sense of the Right Honourable Secretary of State was sufficiently acute to enable him to distinguish between my motives and the nature of my claims, and the transcendant virtues of the dignified moral agent his Lordship had employed for detecting the conspiracy of Thistlewood. I therefore consulted with the gentlemen who, from time to time, had given me the benefit of their opinion and advice, and, on the 9th of October, I empowered Messrs. Finlay and Reddie to settle it on such terms as they were able to obtain. I considered those instructions would have brought the matter immediately to a close, but some other demurrer was put in, which produced an additional though fruitless delay of four months. At last, in February 1821, his Lordship finally determined that a few hundred pounds was a sufficient indemnification for all my losses and sufferings, physical and mental; and as I was completely wearied out, and had fully made up my mind to accept of whatever was offered, it was ultimately settled on those conditions*.

The preceding summary of my personal treatment will not, I trust, be considered too diffuse or unnecessarily extended, when I state that the

* The pertinacious sticklers for economy may allege, that his Lordship acted with a very becoming tenderness and regard for the public purse, in this important national negociation; unless they be illiberal enough to charge him with realizing the proverb, of straining at the gnat while he swallowed the camel. I will only observe that, independent of the pain inflicted upon me by delay, the time taken up, in the negociation, cost me a great deal more money than his Lordship's estimate of the value of the matter in dispute, and that my reiterated remonstrances against that useless waste of time and money were in vain. Should this have the good fortune to come under his Lordship's observation, it will be unnecessary to call to his recollection a passage from an author, from whom I have already quoted, "that it is much easier to ruin a man of principle, than a man of none; for he may be ruined by his scruples, while knavery is supple and can bend;" for, judging from his Lordship's conduct, in my case, it must be inferred that, in the course of his labours for the public benefit, he had been accustomed to come in contact with a description of characters which it would be difficult to bend any lower.

direct and circuitous correspondence in my possession, relative to that part of the subject, would occupy a couple of octavo volumes. Restricting the view, however, to the mere personal question, as it respects so insignificant an individual, it must appear so unimportant as to sink into absolute nothingness; but although it must be viewed as a matter trifling in itself, connected as it is with the conduct of men wielding the destinies of a great and powerful nation, it has been considered, by all who have become acquainted with the particulars, as almost unequalled in the annals of procrastination or tergiversation. A history of the feelings excited, in the various stages, can be of very little importance to the public. I have therefore, as much as possible, abstained from reflection, confining myself to as brief a summary of the facts as was necessary to illustrate the conduct of the different parties; from which, as I formerly observed, every one must draw his own conclusion. I have brooded too long over the real or imaginary wrongs I have suffered, to feel any pleasure in dilating farther upon them, still less am I susceptible of indulging in personal resentments. I shall, therefore, with the few remaining facts I have to allude to, and the few observations I have to make upon this branch of the subject, deviate as little as possible from the same rule.

It will be seen, from the preceding statement, that an evident change of conduct took place towards me, immediately after the session of 1818; first, while the trials, and afterwards, while the discussions in parliament were pending. They were not only profuse in their promises, as to future indemnification, but they accompanied them with an apparently warm expression of feeling for the obloquy I was unjustly exposed to; and, could pecuniary supplies have had any tendency to relieve my mind, the evil might easily have been mitigated, there being, for a time, no want of offers of that kind. With me, however, that was a secondary consideration. My only anxiety was, to have the matter fairly represented; and, in endeavouring to accomplish that object, I exhausted all my own means, and had recourse to my friends before I made any demands upon them. It might be considered presumptuous in me, were I to assert that any of the parties were afraid of disclosures; yet I believe some of them would not, at that time, (if they will now,) have felt much gratified, if a fair portrait of their conduct had been exhibited; and it says little in favour of their justice or generosity, that, as soon as the discussions terminated, and the Indemnity Bill passed, in 1818, it produced a revolution in the whole tone of their feelings. Perhaps, indeed, the Right Honourable Secretary of State was convinced of the truth of the maxim laid down by Julius Cæsar; and, wishing to dispose of the gentlemen who had been so useful to him at home, considered them fit instruments for civilizing Caffrarians and American Indians. If this was his Lordship's view, it was no small proof of his liberality, that he wished to raise me to the dignity of making one of the elements of this delectable compound; for if his protegées could not, like the first crusaders, borrow civilization from the barbarians whom they might be sent to civilize, they could be in no danger of having their morals corrupted; nor did it at all detract from his Lordship's generosity, that he knew popular opinion had placed me in a situation which disabled me from doing justice to my family without his assistance.

In judging of my situation, I can enter into no communing with those who, in forming an estimate of happiness or misery by external circumstances, do not admit that it, in a great measure, depends upon the constitution of the mind; and it would be presumption to doubt that his Lordship possessed a sufficient portion of metaphysical acumen, to reason accurately from that postulate; nor can the justice of his conclusion be reasonably disputed, when it is considered, that the standards to which he could appeal, to take the measure of my mind, were selected from the uncorrupted and incorruptible materials, emanating from one of those prolific seminaries of moral improvement "where all the virtues reign triumphant," a metropolitan prison*. If, therefore, his Lordship committed any mistake, he is entitled to be forgiven, as it must have proceeded from involuntary error, he having reasoned correctly from his premises, although I felt none the less severely the effect of the conclusion.

Constitutionally endowed with an intensity of feeling approaching to morbid sensibility, and acutely alive to the pleasures derived from indulging the social and public affections, I was ill qualified to meet a shock which severed me from the greater portion of my former connexions, or to bear with patience the misconstruction of my motives. At an early age, I had become familiarly acquainted with the condition of the labouring population, in different parts of the United Kingdoms; had observed the evils to which they were then exposed, and anticipated, with no pleasant feelings, many of those which have since overtaken the majority of those engaged in manufactures. As far as the limited sphere of my ope-

* The connexion of government with Castles, Oliver, and Edwards, although formed at different periods, all originated in the Fleet Prison. This fact has been distinctly traced, and could be proved by incontrovertible evidence were it necessary.

rations permitted, I had entered into every scheme considered to have a tendency to avert or mitigate those evils, with a degree of ardour bordering on enthusiasm; believing (as I still do) that everything tending to exalt the great body of the people, as intellectual and moral agents, must eventually promote the true interest of the other classes of the community. At once, however, the whole horizon was overcast. I was denied the power of being susceptible of anything but the lowest, basest, and most selfish feelings. My prospects were blighted; my energies repressed and paralysed; my honourable ambition frustrated, and the future appeared before me one gloomy waste and pathless wilderness. It has been often before remarked, that the pain inflicted by a certain knowledge of the worst event that can take place, is not equal, in intensity, to that resulting from suspense, and on this principle some idea may be formed of my situation, during the four years above alluded to; for, added to all other difficulties, I could form no domestic arrangement, not being certain for one day what the next might bring forth. Perhaps the best illustration I can give of my feelings, will be by a quotation from Spencer's Mother Hubbard's Tale.

> "Full little knowest thou, that hast not tried,
> What hell it is in suing long to bide;
> To lose good days that might be better spent,
> To waste long nights in pensive discontent.
> To speed to-day, to be put back to-morrow;
> To feed on hope, to pine with fear and sorrow;
> To fret thy soul with crosses and with cares;
> To eat thy heart through comfortless despairs."

While I maintained the unequal contest, my internal struggles of mind, and the uncertainty in which I was kept, rendered it impossible for me to attempt any regular business; an evil of no small magnitude, for it gave colour to a belief generally entertained, (which remains on the minds of many until this moment,) that I was employed as an emissary of government, and for that purpose was supported by them. Nothing could more clearly illustrate the force and the fallacy of preconceived opinion, as the exercise of a very ordinary share of penetration might at once have pointed out both its absurdity and impossibility. I resided constantly with my family in the neighbourhood of Edinburgh, a district of country neither involved in the distress nor infected with the opinions which agitated the manufacturing districts. I avoided going to any place where the conduct of public men or public measures was discussed; and the contracted circles of society in which I occasionally intermixed were not selected because they were agreeable to my mind, but because they had neither influence nor interest in public concerns: yet it was of no avail in allaying suspicion. If I condemned any measure adopted by government, it was for the purpose of entrapping. If I approved of any, it was to call forth an opposition that some one might commit himself. If I remained silent, I was an eavesdropper, against whom every one ought to be on his guard; and, although at a distance from the manufacturing districts, it was believed I still maintained a connexion with, and exercised a talismanic influence over them. No mischief could be hatched or plot discovered, without my assistance; for which purpose I was endowed to a certain extent with ubiquity, my presence being necessary in many places at the same time*. Nor has this injustice

* I shall relate, as a specimen, one of the numerous absurd reports of this nature, circulated in the manufacturing districts of Scotland. In October 1821 I went to Ireland on a mercantile speculation, where I was detained a few weeks, and, during my detention, the disturbances which have since, at intervals, agitated the south of that kingdom, commenced in the county of Limerick. It was imme-

been confined to matters having a reference to public measures alone; the same principle has been extended to every attempt I have since made to support my family in private business. In almost every transaction I have been met with suspicion, and the real or imaginary fear of being overreached has been made a sufficient ground of moral justification, for being before hand, where a loophole, quirk, or quibble afforded an opportunity of undue advantage over me.

I could enumerate many instances of this nature, and might be justified in exposing a few of the most palpable; but it is not my intention to insist farther on so ungracious a subject. It can revive no very agreeable recollections, when it comes under the observation of those who have, either publicly or privately, injured me; nor should

diately given out that, as the ferment had ceased in England and Scotland, government had employed me in Ireland, where my arrival had been contemporaneous with insurrections, burnings, and murders, and that my mercantile transactions were only assumed as a cover for my real mission. In passing through Glasgow, on my return home, I found the above report currrently believed, and while there, an incident occurred, illustrative of the unabashed effrontery with which falsehoods are fabricated. A friend, with whom I had passed the previous evening, called at the shop of a merchant, in one of the most public places in the city, where he incidentally met with a mercantile gentleman, just returned from the south of Ireland. After giving some detail of the state of the country, this person professed to have an intimate knowledge of my personal identity, and proceeded to confirm the reports circulated by his own observations, saying he had met me at an inn in the county af Limerick, where I still remained, that he had slept in the same bed-room with me, and related, with the greatest circumstantiality, how I loaded two brace of pistols, and disposed of them and other weapons, beforeI ventured to go to rest. It will be almost unnecessary to add, that I had been no nearer Limerick, or any of the disturbed districts, on that occasion, than the city of Dublin. This was, however, no solitary instance; for I have myself, on several occasions, got a history of my own character, and a description of my person, from people professing to have known me intimately, for many years, who looked foolish enough, when desired to compare the original with the copy.

it diminish the poignancy of that feeling, that I have more pleasure in passing lightly over errors and crimes than in dwelling upon them. There is, however, a point beyond which forbearance is not a virtue, nor do I feel disposed to practise it; and as my family (who were not amenable for my actions) have been equally involved in the consequences, it may superinduce very different measures from those I have yet adopted, or might consider necessary, were I alone the sufferer. It is gratifying to me, that I shall have little more occasion for egotistical reference. I have distinctly brought forward all the parties that were essential to enable the public to form a judgment, and the facts I have adduced must be the *criteria* for censure or eulogy; and upon these I will pass no farther opinion. I should have felt a pleasure in expressing the sense I entertain of many well intended acts of kindness I have received from some of the parties referred to, although, from an ill-judged and mistaken timidity, approaching to pusillanimity, they have, in many points of view, been more injurious to me than if they had proceeded from open and avowed enemies; and, such is the peculiarity of the circumstances, that an imperturbable taciturnity is the best proof I can give of my gratitude, and the most agreeable panegyric I can pay them*.

* I have met with every possible obstruction and discouragement in preparing this narrative for the press, that was in the power of the greater portion of the persons interested. In my correspondence with Mr. Reddie, I fully confided in him, as a private friend; and, in the hurry of overtaking the post, in a few instances, I omitted to take copies of my letters, (retaining only memorandums,) in the most perfect reliance that I could obtain them, if necessary for reference, at any future time. In December last, I apprised him I was going to proceed with this publication, and requested him to furnish me with copies of those letters, (amounting only to six,) as I was exceedingly anxious to make no misstatement or omission. In reply, he informed me, *he had*

I have trespassed long upon the patience of my readers with individual consequences, yet it may satisfy the curiosity of some and, in other respects, may not be without its use; not because I consider my individuality of any public importance, but, as we know nothing certain of the future but by reasoning from the past, it may be a lesson to those that follow after. Society has too few opportunities of ascertaining the secret springs that move in such transactions as I have described, the agents having no desire that either their real motives or actions should be known. Yet it is only by an extensive knowledge of past events we can acquire that kind of prescience which enables us, in many cases, to foretell what will again happen, and to use our prudence to guard against it. In a general point of view, few accidents in political

consulted with Mr. Finlay, and, however little disposed he might otherwise be to retain the letters, *he apprehended he would be wanting in his official duty, and expose himself to the just censure of government, were he to give them up for the purpose of promoting any publication, without previous permission from the Secretary of State for the Home Department, or the law officers of the crown.* I am at a loss to account for Mr. Reddie's conduct in this instance, he having, at a former period, made a voluntary tender of those letters, and any other information that might be useful, when required; but *whoever*, or whatever, may have been the cause, I, nevertheless, consider him one of the most estimable men I have ever met. In every other respect I experienced the same humane and amiable disposition, the same sympathy and benevolence, the same candour and justice, that characterized his conduct in all the public measures upon which I had an opportunity of making observations. He sedulously endeavoured to impress upon the attention of government, that the measures pursued had utterly ruined all my prospects, and I do not the less highly estimate his unremitting attention and unwearied perseverance, to induce them to do me justice, that all his efforts proved abortive, for he acted consistently throughout, in which respect he stood alone. The letters alluded to were of no great consequence; but it is fortunate that, in conducting my correspondence, I trusted little to future contingencies, as I could not now command a single document by the courtesy of any of the parties interested.

affairs are unique, the seeds of most of them are sown in the wide field of universal nature, and will produce similar fruit, at periods more or less remote. If, indeed, civilized society ever exhibited a pure and perfect anomaly to which no parallel can be produced, either in the ages that are past or the present, it is the existing state of society in this country; and if any dependence is to be placed on the opinions of those who have the most extensive means of practical observation, we are, at present, enjoying only a temporary and deceitful calm. In proportion as a combination of new powers are extending our manufacturing system with unexampled rapidity, conducted on a principle, the direct tendencies of which are to debase the mass of productive labourers, so in proportion will the first reaction produce a scene of misery, appalling beyond all former precedent. Similar causes may, therefore, be expected to produce similar results; and, if any portion of the pending evil can be averted, by pointing out the errors committed during the past ferment, some part of my design will be accomplished.

No statement of facts or general reasoning, from so humble a source, will have much influence on the conduct of statesmen, who are generally the last to learn or improve. Government, by far the most important branch of the science of morals, has hitherto been conducted on the principle, that the bulk of mankind are incapable of distinguishing right from wrong, and physical coercion is the instrument used, instead of operating on the moral sympathies. On that assumption mysticism has been universally resorted to, as if, as Dean Swift has remarked, there were something so abstruse and profound in politics, that men of plain, honest sense could not arrive at; while, in point of fact, men are frequently placed in situations that give them an influence over the destinies of nations, whose intellectual endowments and knowledge of the habits and feelings of the bulk of society are so superficial as scarcely to entitle them to hold the rank or discharge the duties of village magistrates. Judging from past experience, however, it is not at all probable that any useful or lasting impression can be made upon that class of men; from age to age, they have proceeded, from blunder to blunder, on the dogmatical assumption of their own superiority, their errors chiefly resulting from being unconscious of their ignorance. Amelioration is therefore only to be expected from a more general diffusion of knowledge amongst the body of the people, which, by enabling them to take a comprehensive view of their relative situation, may prevent them, when involved in distress, from being misled by the ignorant (though perhaps well meaning) enthusiast, or duped by the designing. Until the people acquire that so necessary and so desirable portion of information and clearness of perception, nothing could be of more utility than a complete elucidation of the deceptions they practised upon each other; and the empirical expedients of government, from the end of 1816 to the conviction of Thistlewood and his associates, and those who suffered for high treason in Scotland, in 1820. The general result may be sufficient for the philosopher and future historian, but the details would be useful and important to the labouring classes, and might assist in preventing a repetition of former errors. Although I had no connexion with any party or with any of the transactions subsequent to 1817, I was not an inattentive observer of passing events; and, in addition to what I then learned, from various sources, since the ferment subsided, I have been at considerable pains to obtain information from several of the prominent actors, both in England and Scotland. I will not attempt to enter into a minute detail; but as neither government nor its agents, nor the party opposed to them, are likely to become the historians of their own delinquencies, I shall endeavour to give a brief sketch of the leading circumstances, believing that the facts and opinions may be confidently relied on.

It must be borne in mind, that the primary cause of discontent and disaffection was positive suffering; the subsequent errors, committed by the different parties, being only proximate and secondary aggravations of the evil. The immediate cause of the distress may be shortly defined: it was produced by a cessation of demand for British products, equal to the amount of the surplus capital, which, during the war, was annually invested in loans to government; who, in foreign subsidies, payment of the army, navy, and other expenses, circulated bills, which could only be paid by the products of our own industry, the interest of the capital so advanced being provided for by taxes imposed to a corresponding amount, as a security for annuities to the lenders from the permanent revenue. The first error committed by government was, in our foreign policy, in not making a proper use of the commanding situation we occupied at the general peace, to secure commercial advantages from the other states of Europe; which might, in some measure, have counteracted the cessation of demand created by loans being no longer required, admitting we had been able to continue such an improvident expenditure. Our merchants also, for some time unaware of the consequences, continued to export to an equal amount as formerly, (although there was no possibility of obtaining equivalents,) until every market was glutted, which produced a corresponding depreciation in value, lessened the demand and lowered the price of labour on the same ratio, and brought bankruptcy and ruin upon the immediate holders of our products. This depreciating principle extended itself until it involved the mass of productive labourers in misery, and the privations to which they were compelled to submit reacted upon all classes, by causing an enormous diminution of the home consumption of all agricultural, manufactured and foreign productions.

It is true it was not in the power of government to retrace their steps, or avert all the evils consequent on so expensive and (to the extent to which it was carried) so impolitic a war: but, the first error once committed, it was their obvious, imperative and paramount duty, in the midst of such a complicated scene of misery, to adopt every possible method of conciliation, a virtue for which the statesman who, at the time had the chief sway in our councils, was never eminently conspicuous. Unfortunately for society (if not for himself) his education was completed and his character formed in a school and in a country where centuries of misgovernment had familiarized a dominant faction with every species of oppression. Although admitted to be courteous and kind in private life, his situation had been most unfavourable for forming just conceptions of government, or for developing the milder public virtues; and when the people, goaded by their sufferings, gave vent to their feelings in loud and general complaints, in his public character he treated them with haughty derision and supercilious contempt. Cajoled and, at the same time, duped by the Holy Legitimates, he was too highly elated with the imaginary success of his foreign policy to condescend to listen to the complaints of a British *canaille,* and from a Cabinet, with a person at its head, entertaining such sentiments, no conciliatory measures were to be expected. It was necessary, however, to put down the presumptuous and audacious clamour, and the Suspension of the Habeas Corpus Act naturally presented itself as the best means for accomplishing that object. The example set by the dispensers of power and emolument is always too contagious not to be imitated; and the same spirit was immediately infused into, and the same tone of uncompromising haughty overbearing insolence assumed by, the subordinate satellites of government, in the greater portion of the districts where the distress was most prevalent.

It is an acknowledged axiom, in the history of human passions, that men will generally submit with more patience to real injuries than contemptuous or reproachful epithets; and the contumelious arrogance with which the people were treated had a powerful tendency to arouse their resentment, and make them feel their degradation more acutely*. I have already described the effects of this policy, during the years 1816 and 1817, in Scotland, which may be taken as an epitome of the feelings of the people in other parts of the country. Contrary to the falsely assumed principle and averments in the reports of the parliamentary committees, it is now a well-ascertained fact, that neither then, nor during the subsequent years, was there any very extensive or very perfectly arranged plan of organization. The persons who deceived themselves and misled the people

* Mr. Burke's epithet, of swinish multitude, has never been forgotten nor forgiven; and the Marquis of Londonderry's assertion, that the people betrayed an ignorant impatience of taxation, has also become a common proverb.

acted on the presumption, that the government was so imbecile and unpopular, and the discontent so general, that the people only required to be put in motion to overturn it with facility, and not on any regular or well-digested scheme of communication, which was the revolving axis of all their delusions. The view held out to the country, and upon which parliament legislated, when they passed the Suspension Bill in 1817, was, that a general system of affiliation had been established, for the purpose of producing a revolutionary movement, the focus of which was in London, the ramifications extending through all the manufacturing counties of England and Scotland. Now I have clearly shown, that the party accused in Scotland was completely insulated, nor was there more truth in the allegation, as it respected the metropolis and the manufacturing counties in England. It is true that committees were formed in most of the towns, who were corresponding with each other for the purpose of promoting parliamentary reform; but their measures were all open, the persons engaged having neither the hope nor the design of effecting it by violence. The leaders of the riots at the Spafield Meeting, on the 2d of December, 1816, had no regular correspondence with any of the provinces, and knew nothing of their condition, except from the public reports, and loose and general rumour. There were, indeed, but very few persons in the secret of those proceedings, and that few certainly not possessing ability, character, or influence to take a comprehensive view of the state of the country, or of conducting any extensive chain of operations. They believed the government to be so odious and the labouring population involved in such misery, that they were ripe for revolt and ready to go any length. The public meetings were held in the metropolis, to operate on their passions, but without any preconcerted plan with any other part of the country. They considered, with the assistance of those they could select from the motley groups they assembled, that the Bank and the Tower could be carried by a *coup de main*, which would be a signal for a general insurrection, when they would be joined by such a multitude as would lay the government prostrate, as if by magic.

Such is the real history of that transaction, which, when we examine it by the test of its practicability, resembles the reveries of some of the ideal emperors and kings, whose power of locomotion extends no farther than the will of their keepers, or the boundary-wall of a madhouse; the scheme being as rational and as likely to succeed, as if a fishing-boat had attempted to carry by escalade the fortress of Gibraltar, with all its garrison on the alert. By endeavouring to magnify these injudicious and culpable, but puerile attempts, (which certainly ought to have been prevented, or otherwise punished,) and gravely proceeding against the actors for high treason, the prosecutors brought defeat and disgrace upon themselves, gave influence and importance to insignificance, and placed an English minister in the humiliating situation of disputing pre-eminence with a journeyman shoemaker. It is not alleged, by the persons engaged in these transactions, that *Castles* (who figured on the trial as a witness for the crown) was possessed of ability to influence their proceedings, but there is no doubt whatever that government was previously acquainted with their intention; and, without going the length of charging their emissaries with direct instigation, it cannot be denied that, with that knowledge, they were highly culpable for allowing the overt acts of riot to be committed.

Such was the extent of treason and organization, previous to the mission of Oliver into the country; the blanket expedition from Manchester, and the movement in the neighbourhood of Huddersfield being mere local ebullitions, so trifling in their nature, that the parties brought to trial were acquitted even of riot. It is not at all probable that a faithfully-detailed account of Oliver's proceedings will ever be laid before the public, as he is not likely to be ambitious of becoming his own biographer, admitting credit could be attached to his statements. It is questionable, also, if in many instances his employers had any other means of ascertaining how he conducted himself, but from his own reports; and, on the other hand, those who betrayed themselves to him, or were betrayed by him into improper actions or expressions, cannot give a statement of particulars, without at the same time exposing the impropriety of their own conduct. Again; where he did not fully succeed, or where the parties tampered with were not so far committed as to render the disclosure dangerous or dishonourable, the probability is, that the statements put forth were accompanied with such a portion of colouring as to make him appear worse than he was in reality. Nothing, therefore, but a general conclusion can be drawn with propriety: the facts and presumptions are, however, sufficiently strong and numerous to point out clearly, that the policy of employing such a person, in such a manner, was injudicious and improper, and attended with the most pernicious consequences.

From the Fleet Prison he first commenced his operations in London, where he introduced himself to a number of persons who were known to be friendly to parliamentary reform, also to Dr. Watson, Thistlewood, and others, who had influence among the populace, and for some time attended their meetings. Having a tolerable address, and a manner rather prepossessing, he succeeded in insinuating himself so far into their confidence as to answer the purpose he had in view. Amongst others, he got introduced to Mr. Mitchell, who had been deputed from Lancashire to attend a reform meeting in London, and professing the greatest zeal for the cause, he proposed that they should, together, visit some of the towns in the country, for the purpose of ascertaining more particularly how they stood affected. Under that pretext he proceeded first to Birmingham, in company with Mitchell, where he spent some time, and was introduced to a number of the friends of reform in that place. He however made no farther impression at Birmingham, than obtaining the names of their friends in the adjacent towns and villages; and, as he proceeded, the particular references he could make, from persons in one place to those in another, served as an introduction, and also as a voucher that he might be fully depended upon, as a friend of the popular cause. In that manner he proceeded from place to place, through a number of the manufacturing districts; but it is unnecessary to trace him through the mazes of his various missions, or to condescend upon particular acts of instigation, the broad and general fact being sufficiently established and sufficiently conclusive. That he gave out that he was deputed by the popular party in London, who were convinced that neither reform nor relief was to be expected, unless it could be obtained by force; that, under that conviction, they had men and arms provided to a large amount in the metropolis, ready to act at a moment's notice, and that they only waited for a general insurrectionary movement in the country districts to insure certain success. Admitting, therefore, there were no local instigation whatever, and supposing a man in such circumstances to be otherwise immaculate, the effect of such a representation, on the minds of a starving population, could not fail to be pernicious, and the wonder rather is, that the empyrosis was not more general*. It however led to the arrest of a number of persons, in various parts of the country, under the operation of the Suspension Bill, and at length to the mock insurrection in Derbyshire, which terminated in the trial, conviction and execution of Brandreth and his associates, and also in the exposure of Oliver.

When these convictions took place at Derby, the impolitic conduct of the ministry was again most palpable. However injurious political crimes may be to the interest of society, or however criminal and absurd an attempt against the established government, the bulk of the people are always disposed to consider the sufferers as martys, it being exceedingly difficult to impress them with a belief that they are accompanied with moral turpitude. But here the belief was universal that, although the accused parties were legally or technically guilty of treason, they had been entrapped and directly instigated to the crime, by an emissary of government. Admitting, therefore, it had been thought proper to bring them to trial, to

* Early in June, and a short time prior to the disturbances in Derbyshire, Mr. Parker, a magistrate at Sheffield, informed Lord Sidmouth, that a Mr. Oliver, a person representing himself as deputed by the reformers in London, was going round that town and neighbourhood, instigating the people by the most inflammatory language. His Lordship, in reply, informed Mr. Parker, that Oliver was an agent of his own, and to take no notice of him; but Mr. Parker immediately requested him to be withdrawn, pledging himself and assuring his Lordship, that there was no danger of the people being guilty of any impropriety, if no person came to interfere with them.

show that, *by law*, even instigation is no justification for crime, the moment a conviction was obtained there, they ought to have stopped. It was, then, a clearly obvious and politic case for the interposition of the royal mercy; and never, in this age, could the dispensing power of the crown have been more judiciously exercised. Never was there a better opportunity for rendering the government popular, counteracting the influence of former errors, and showing the people that the object was to make them desist from such foolish and impracticable attempts, and not to inflict sanguinary or vindictive punishment. Nor could a pardon of the culprits have been attended with any future hazard. We were not living in a state of society where, as a matter of policy, a government may lay hold upon any pretext to dispose of a factious, turbulent nobleman. The persons were so insignificant, that their release could have been attended with no future danger, and the well-timed act of clemency would have had a superior effect upon the minds of the people to a thousand executions. Matters of the kind are not to be estimated by the mere sacrifice of individual life, in which point of view it is comparatively unimportant. The pain of the immediate sufferers is very soon past, and the remembrance and the loss are soon confined to their relatives and friends; for, as individuals, they are soon forgotten by the rest of society; but the act of public injustice, to which they may fall victims, makes a deeper and more lasting impression, and frequently prevents obscurity from sinking into oblivion. Those executions at Derby, added to the previous trials for treason, and their resisting every attempt at inquiry, summed up the blunders of the ministry in 1817; inflicted a wound and completed a breach that has not yet been healed, by maturing those rancorous feelings in the minds of the labouring population, which were previously in a state of adolescence; gave an influence and ascendancy to speaking and writing demagogues, who, deceiving themselves and one another, kept the country in commotion for several years, threw obstructions in the way of obtaining any rational amelioration in the representation, and terminated in the useless immolation of more lives, and a dangerous inroad upon the constitution.

A temporary calm succeeded the ebullitions of 1817, occasioned partly by a hope, for some time indulged, that parliament would institute an inquiry into the obnoxious measures, and partly by an increased demand and very partial advance on the price of labour in some of the larger branches of our manufactures. This calm was, however, illusory and evanescent; coercion only produced a submission which, instead of subduing, infused a spirit of greater implacability, and the elements, that were raised to the surface by the tempest, became too buoyant and subtle to remain long in a state of inactivity. The more wise, temperate and prudent part of the advocates for parliamentary reform, afraid, on the one hand, that the people were disposed to drive things to extremities, and, on the other, accused by the supporters of the ministry as the abettors of revolution, considering the time unpropitious for pressing that question farther, progressively ceased to make any active exertion in the cause. This comprised the most respectable and influential class, so that the future attempts were chiefly confined to the labouring population, upon a principle which would virtually effect a revolution, not a reform, of the present system of representation. The persons who henceforth obtained an uncontrolled ascendancy not being the most enlightened, or capable of directing them to any useful or practicable result, gave full swing to their passions and enmity against the government, availing themselves of every method and opportunity of inflaming the people's minds. After the expiration of the Suspension Bill in 1818, the ferment was renewed, and kept up by means of public meetings and inflammatory harangues, the example being set by the party in the metropolis, which soon became contagious, and again extended itself into all the manufacturing counties in both kingdoms. There was, however, no regular cohesion of the parts of this system, until towards the end of 1818, when union societies began to be formed in the respective towns, and secret communications were established by delegates, who practised the grossest deceptions upon each other, and propagated delusions respecting the amount of their number and the extent of their resources. The plan proposed by the persons who now took the lead was, to work upon the minds of the people, and at the same time distract and divide the attention of government, by holding simultaneous meetings, in various parts of the country. Conjoined with which measure, they were to fabricate or purchase arms, to the extent of their means, and, as far as practicable, acquire a knowledge of their use, by secret nocturnal military trainings; trusting that the chapter of accidents would furnish a favourable opportunity for ulterior operations.—This sage scheme was successfully put in practice, as far as respected the public meetings; the military trainings were also partially carried on in some of the country districts, both anterior and posterior to the meeting at Manchester, on the 16th of August, 1819, which may be considered the next great epoch in this dangerous, absurd, impolitic, and tragical drama of fooleries. Too few facts are yet known to decide, with certainty, as to who was the immediate cause of the catastrophe at Manchester; neither the coroner's inquest nor Mr. Hunt's trial throwing any light upon the secret springs which moved it. It is impossible, however, to command language sufficiently strong to convey an adequate idea of reprobation against the conduct of government for quashing all inquiry into that stain upon our national annals. Whether it was in consequence of an order from a minister of state, or the act of a self-willed local magistracy; whether it was an error in judgment, or the effect of design; whether it was caused by radicals, whigs, or ultra tories humanity, public justice and sound policy demanded, that the delinquents should not be screened; that a free and unshackled inquiry should take place, by a tribunal above the influence of local prejudice; an inquiry which could only have been made, with propriety, by the great council of the nation; and that it was not so made, is little to the honour of the majority of that august assembly. A judge and jury afterwards decided, that the meeting had assembled for an illegal purpose, from which it was inferred, that the attack, made upon it by the military, was justifiable, although no overt illegal act had yet been committed. But, granting that assumption, it only proves that the meeting ought to have been prevented. At the last the crime only existed in and was constituted by intention; and the shade of difference is very slight, where there is proof of an intention to meet for an illegal purpose, and where the parties have actually met, without having committed any overt act, and is equally liable to punishment. It was, therefore, the duty of the magistrates to prevent the assembly, by arresting the leaders and all who were instrumental in calling it. This they might easily have done, on some of the preceding days, and adopted measures of precaution for preventing disturbance. They were as fully aware of the real intention, prior to the meeting, as after it had taken place; the depositions then taken, being a mere flimsy pretext, and no justification for the *manner* in which the wanton, unnecessary, and even unsoldierlike attack was made upon the infatuated multitude*.

Were it not for the utility arising from holding up such a scene to view as a beacon, to be avoided in future, every Briton, who has one spark of the *amor patria,* must feel anxious that it should be no longer held in remembrance, but blotted from the pages of our history. Had it been the cool and deliberate intention of the ministry to bring all the odium and unpopularity on their measures, which might have been divided by the errors of the opposing parties, they could not have done it

* The public will probably never learn more than is already known, of the cause of the error against sound sense and sound policy, committed by the magistrates at Manchester, but the following statement of facts, which occurred on the other side, antecedent to the meeting, may not be uninteresting. Mr. Hunt, at some of the meetings in the metropolis, had asserted, in no very measured or equivocal language, that no efficient reform was to be obtained unless it was effected by force. Such a declaration, coming from *such authority,* had its due weight upon the minds of the people, who, not doubting his sincerity, believed the proper time had arrived for making the experiment. They considered too, that he, who had fought their battles in so bold and undaunted a manner on the hustings, must also be best qualified to lead them into the field; and, with this view, he was invited to preside at the meeting at Manchester. On his arrival, the committee informed him, that as the time for action had arrived, everything was prepared for his reception in Manchester; that two deputies were sent to about thirty of the neighbouring towns, with instructions for the people to attend the meeting armed; and, agreeable to his former declaration, they expected he was come to fight as well as make speeches. Mr. Hunt, however, considering matters not quite ripe for going

more successfully. By resisting all inquiry into this nefarious transaction, they gave something like a national, though meteoric, importance to a turbulent demagogue and pseudo politician who, from that time, affected to despise and look down upon the party as minions, to whom he was chiefly indebted for his previous notoriety. The high hand with which everything was thus carried, soon produced its corresponding fruits, by stimulating a set of reckless, desperate men to the last act of the tragedy; and it appears to have been the future policy of government, to allow them fully to commit themselves. The limits I have prescribed for myself not allowing me to go into any lengthened detail of what followed, I shall confine myself briefly to such circumstances as have not previously been laid before the public in any connected form.

It was in London, and under the very eye of government, that the delusion was kept up, which had the chief influence in misleading the popu-

so far, and being afraid of the consequences that might result from a display of his rabid racy eloquence, under such ticklish circumstances, refused to preside, and threatened to leave the town immediately, unless the order for arming was recalled. A good deal of altercation and recrimination followed, but it was at length agreed, that a second deputation should be sent to countermand the order, with as much celerity as possible. The two deputations after some time, met together, when their conflicting orders created much confusion, the people not knowing which to obey, and some few of them actually did attend the meeting with such arms as they had in their possession. These consisted chiefly of a kind of pole, in the form of a walking-stick, on the end of which a pike or piece of sharpened iron could be affixed, removable at pleasure. The most material part of those circumstances was not unknown to the local authorities, prior to the meeting; but it may with propriety be inquired, how far the imprudent conduct and inflammatory language of Mr. Hunt had contributed to work up the people's minds to such a pitch. How far he was ignorant of the consequences of such language, or still more culpable, if he acted so from design; in fine, how far he divides the blame and is answerable with the magistrates and yeomanry for the outrage on public feeling and the widows and orphans made by the massacre at Manchester.

lation in the manufacturing districts; and, from its nature, bears the strongest evidence of want of vigilance, capability, or sincerity to put an end to it. Dr. Watson, Thistlewood, and a very few others, were the inventors and executors of the scheme, which was simply as follows: They met at a public-house, and collected as many of the unemployed, idle, and dissolute of the working classes, from all quarters of London, as they were able to procure; the more indigent and illiterate the better. This assemblage, by way of eminence, was designated the Committee of Two Hundred, being self-elected, self-named, and having no other constituents than misery and distress; for it is a fact, worthy the most particular attention, that at no period, during the highest degree of ferment, were there any regularly organized associations in London. An attempt was made, early in 1819, to consolidate them into union societies, when some few oaths of secrecy were administered; but it proved completely abortive, even the nominal members never exceeding from three to four hundred, and it was almost immediately abandoned. The Committee of *Two Hundred, constituted as above described,* was, therefore, the real talisman; they being held up as the representatives of an immensely numerous and powerful body, that nowhere existed but in imagination, or perhaps in the reports of some of the government emissaries. By their means were all the public meetings got up; and to no less dignified materials is Hunt indebted for all his metropolitan celebrity.

When the feelings of all classes were wrought up to the highest pitch, by the transactions at Manchester, another reaction (caused by an excess of exportation during the preceding year) had involved the manufacturing districts in the greatest distress. Thousands were thrown out of employment, and the price of labour was, in many instances, reduced even below the point it had reached in 1816-17. At the same time, the ministerial papers, to palliate and justify the outrage at Manchester, daily, but most erroneously and falsely, asserted, that secret societies and revolutionary associations existed in London to a great and alarming extent. The labouring population, in the manufacturing districts, relying on the correctness of those representations, after ineffectually exhausting every local expedient to obtain relief, considered there was no alternative but to strike at the root of the evil, by following the example of their metropolitan brethren, who, they believed, had far outstripped them in the race of regeneration. In Scotland, where parochial assessments do not exist to an extent to operate even as a palliative in such an emergency, the distress was greater than in any part of England; added to which, was the rooted hatred against the government, produced by the belief, that the people had been entrapped into the conspiracy in 1816-17. The embryo of an association was formed in Glasgow, and a communication opened with London, by letter, which led to a regular correspondence; and, in two months, the organization was ramified by delegation, into the greater part of the manufacturing towns in the west of Scotland, and also into part of the counties of York and Lancaster. This connexion was formed with Thistlewood and his party; for, in consequence of the eclat with which Hunt was received, on his triumphant entry into London, after the affair at Manchester, considering he could then occupy higher ground, he broke with his former associates, and, as an apology for his defection, charged Thistlewood with being a spy of the government. In the manufacturing districts the organization was formed strictly on the model of the Irish in 1798 (an outline of which I have given in page 77); the minor details were, indeed, chiefly concocted and carried into execution by emigrants, who had been engaged in that rebellion in Ireland. After the passing of the Six Acts, in November 1819, when they could no longer hold public meetings, the secret organization was extended with great rapidity in Scotland. Central or select committees, consisting of only three persons, had the control over a district of a certain extent, who received all communications; and, implicit confidence being placed in them, they could convey or withhold any information they thought proper. A *constitutional* reform, on the basis of universal suffrage and annual parliaments, was the ostensible pretence; but it was soon assumed and avowed, that it was only to be obtained by compulsion; and they made every preparation in their power to carry it into execution. The precise time Thistlewood first meditated the blow he intended to strike, or by what, or by whom incited*, must be, in some measure, left to conjecture; but much anxiety prevailed at the time, and it has created much speculation since, whether it was a mere in-

* Although Thistlewood's private circumstances were sufficiently desperate to render him reckless, many are of opinion, that a heated imagination and mistaken zeal have obtained for him the name of an assassin instead of a patriot. Some who knew him well, affirm, that the charge made against him by Hunt, that he was employed by government, made a deep impression on his mind; and that, from that time, he seemed embued with an opinion, that he should perform some bold and daring act to wipe away the imputation. Be it, however, as it may, a much more trifling incident has been frequently known to give the human mind a determinate and immovable bias. It may be recollected that, after the rupture with Hunt, he went upon a mission to Manchester; and, in the dispute that occurred, Hunt asserted, that he had traced the money, to defray the expense of the journey, to the Treasury; when it was well known to all the party, that he had sold and pledged a part of his books for the purpose.

sulated act of his own, or only part of a more extended plan of operations. On positive evidence, an end can be put to all ambiguity on that point. The select committees had been some time generally apprised, that an important and decisive measure was contemplated by the *committee* in London; and, when he had taken his final resolution, he acquainted them, that ten days posterior, the news of a desperate stroke against their enemies would reach them. To summon all their host, have the people prepared to seize their lost rights, and be ready to follow up victory as they should be farther instructed. No particulars of the nature of the design were communicated; but, on receipt of the intelligence, the committees implicitly obeyed; delegates were dispatched in all directions, and all was whisper and conjecture. The select committee at Glasgow sat for two days and nights, issuing orders and receiving information of the effect of these efforts; and, on the night of the 22d of February, 1820, the day previous to the arrests in Cato-street, a general congress of delegates, from all the connexion in Scotland, was held a few miles from Paisley. There they invoked the spirit of Wallace, swore fidelity to each other, dispatched a delegate to the north of England, and returned to their homes, scarcely breathing with anxiety for the arrival of every successive post.

When the account of the fate of Thistlewood and his party at last reached them, they were staggered and confounded; some slight commotion followed, around Glasgow, but as there was no simultaneous movement, as was expected, in the north of England, it soon subsided. It is not a little remarkable, that, although government distinctly knew (if their emissaries did not abet) all Thistlewood's proceedings in London, that they had no accurate knowledge of the nature or extent of his connexion with the country. The local authorities were aware that, for some days, scouts were sent from the different towns, who manifested great anxiety, on the arrival of the mails, but they knew nothing more; and those who were leaders, up to that date, successfully eluded their vigilance, and escaped detection. The snare into which Thistlewood and his associates had fallen, and their pending fate, the particulars of which are already known, did not put an end to the infatuation. In Scotland, when the leaders, shuddering on the brink of the precipice, from which they had so narrowly escaped, hesitated and stood aloof, new committees were chosen. Each successive change of leaders brought forward men of a lower grade, with less of intellect, but still more reckless than their predecessors. Only fearless desperation being now in requisition, all caution was laid aside, and emissaries, employed by the magistrates, found easy access amongst them. Some of those emissaries were found amongst their own party; by which means the outline of their future plans became perfectly known to government; but the policy adopted, was to allow them to proceed.

The month of March was spent in concocting a plan of insurrection with the northern counties of England, to operate as a diversion in favour of the metropolis; where, notwithstanding the exposure of the paucity of numbers and the insignificance of Thistlewood's party, they foolishly imagined there were myriads ready to act with them. The first of April being fixed upon for carrying the design into execution, orders were issued, that all the people should then abstain from labour until they obtained a redress of grievances, and, by means of threats and intimidation, they forced the greater part of the labouring population to comply. On the morning of the above day, a printed proclamation, purporting to emanate from a provisional committee of government, was posted on the walls in Glasgow and some of the adjacent towns and villages, pointing out the necessity for a change of measures, and calling the people to arms, to revolutionize the government*. The surrounding districts were thrown into great alarm, and by collecting crowds and circulating reports, in one place, that the people were in arms, in another they induced a few ignorant, foolish men (in reality the dupes of the others) to commit overt acts, by displaying banners, and, in one or two instances, attempting to seize arms, which exposed them to a formal charge of treason and rebellion. Not without the strongest suspicion of having been, in the first instance, led by an emissary of the magistrates, all the forces that could be assembled left Glasgow for the purpose of storming the Carron iron-works, to get possession of some field

* A report was circulated, which has since been gravely chronicled, as a matter of history, that this proclamation was the production of a person of the name of Franklin, *alias* Fletcher, who was, in September following, charged at Bow-street office with circulating seditious hand-bills for the purpose of exciting disturbances in the metropolis. He was supposed to be connected with government, and to have carried on the practice for years, and the presumptions against him are strong. Being kept in custody by one magistrate, he was set at liberty by another, when he immediately absconded, and the Grand Jury of the county of Middlesex afterward found a true bill against him for high treason. But whatever may have been the delinquencies of government, and they deserve to be branded with eternal infamy, if they countenanced any such nefarious and contemptible practices, they stand acquitted of all blame in this matter. Now, when all danger is past, it may be stated, on unquestionable authority, that the proclamation was both drawn up and printed in Glasgow, and certainly by persons the reverse of having any connexion with government, although they had the good fortune to escape. Charges of that nature ought to be always attended to with caution, the policy of giving currency to such reports, by the immediate actors, being obvious; for, allowing the

pieces, but were met on the way by *twelve* dragoons, who, after exchanging a few shots, made them all prisoners. This, by way of eminence, was called the *battle* of Bonnymuir, which finally crushed the insurrection. Only a very slight commotion, in a few places in the north of England, accompanied this visionary attempt at national regeneration in Scotland; which, when too late, undeceived the deluded men, and at the same time gave the strongest evidence of the falsity and futility of the averments of the ministry, that the bulk of the labouring population were bent on revolution. No departure, however, took place from the former policy: a special commission was appointed, and, after the conspiracy was completely broken up, true bills for high treason were found against near one hundred persons, in the counties of Lanark, Air, Renfrew, and Stirling. Of these near thirty were convicted, and, to the disgrace of an age that boasts of its civilization, three of them were executed with all the disgusting formalities of barbarism, and the remainder transported*.

author to have been proud of his production, like authors of more note, he could not be unconscious of the advantage to be derived from remaining incognito, and making the publication anonymous. The impositions practised on the public were not, perhaps, so mischievous in their consequences, nor so perversely wicked, as those they practised on their own adherents, an instance of which occurred, at this time, in Glasgow, deserving the severest reprobation. On the return of a delegate, sent to the north of England to ascertain their condition and urge on the insurrection, he faithfully reported to the select committee that, when it had come to the point, the number of their friends was so small, that they could make no impression on the body of the people. On receiving this information, the committee enjoined him to secresy, said they were too far committed to retract, and immediately caused reports to be circulated, that all the manufacturing counties in England were in arms; by those means the few that made any demonstration were duped and sacrificed; for, mad as they certainly were, they never would have made such an attempt, had they not expected a simultaneous effort in England.

* One of these, a poor old man, an operative weaver, and the

In reviewing those proceedings, it is apparent, that the conduct of few of the parties entitle them to the approbation of enlightened, wise, and good men; yet it is difficult accurately to point out all the faults committed, and award each their due portion of blame. On the part of government, from the commencement to the close, their errors may be summed up in one sentence; a want of conciliation, and making punishment, not prevention, the ultimate end and aim of all their measures; a line of policy founded on such false data, that it never can lead to any permanent, good, or beneficial result. By admitting the principle of tyrannicide, we break down the chief bulwark and safeguard of society, and set every man in arms against his own brother. Yet it is questionable, even in the case of Thistlewood and his associates, (certainly, in a moral point of view, the least objectionable of all the capital punishments inflicted,) if the means adopted did not destroy all the salutary effects that such an example could have

simple inhabitant of a country village, little to the honour of government and much less for any utility by way of example, (his fate exciting universal commiseration,) was executed at Glasgow. When one of the false reports was circulated, that the country was all in arms, he had been almost forced from his home by a party of men, with whom he proceeded to a farmhouse, where he was well known, where they took possession of a fowlingpiece, which was afterwards returned. This was all the charge against him, but the true cause of that useless immolation was as follows:—Although Glasgow was the focus of all the mischief, they could lay hold of no other person who had committed any overt act within the county; proceeding, therefore, on the ordinary principle, that if people will not follow virtue for its own reward, they will be terrified from the commission of crime by the example of sanguinary punishment, it was considered necessary to have at least one victim sacrificed as near as possible to the hot-bed of radicalism. Paisley would have answered the purpose nearly as well, but there the firmness of a juryman prevented any conviction, which decided the fate of poor Wilson, and gave an additional evidence, if any more were wanting, that even the most depraved of mankind will never be made wiser or better by such disgusting exhibitions, as it produced an effect exactly opposite to what was intended.

been expected to produce on the minds of the people. Nor, to support this hypothesis, is it necessary to assume, that that unhappy man was instigated to the crime he intended to commit, by any emissary of government. It may be granted, he had a mind so waywardly constituted, as neither to be urged on nor moved from its fixed and determinate purpose, by any external influence; still, it cannot be denied, that he was deliberately led, bound hand and foot, to his fate, while the safety of society might have been better secured by an earlier stop being put to his career, and by disposing of him in a different manner.

The errors, however, did not all lie on that side; there were others, either through ignorance of the effect which their lucubrations must inevitably have produced, or from a much baser motive, no less guilty. The press has, with justice, been denominated a new power in the present state of society; and, like every other species of power, the good or bad effects produced by it must exclusively depend upon the manner of its direction. It may, therefore, be asked, who were the friends of rational liberty? Was it the conductors of that part of the periodical press, who, for the paltry and contemptible consideration of pecuniary emolument, by the sale of their productions, goaded on and inflamed the minds of the people, with abstract cabalistic nostrums, while smarting under the lash of privation and misery, and then basely deserted them, on the edge of the precipice, saying, now you are going too far, I will not longer share the danger? As if they could sit on the whirlwind and direct the storm, make the waves of the ocean obey them, or fix a boundary to the mighty waters, when agitated by all the terrors of the hurricane. Much less guilty were those unfortunate men, who expiated their errors on a scaffold; whose untimely fate must draw the tear of pity from the eye of the benevolent, although not intitled to rank as martyrs to an enlightened patriotism, but as the victims of an absurd delusion.

The conduct of the whig aristocracy, both in and out of parliament, was also far from blameless, during these ferments. When all parties ought to have coalesced, in adopting joint measures, for the relief of the people, their latent love of power made them enjoy, with self-complacency and self-gratulation, the embarrassment of their opponents, hoping it would lead to their own elevation; and, in accordance with this view, that part of the press, which was under their influence, was decidedly too long in attempting to stem the torrent of mendacious opinion. The radical error of the manufacturing population consisted in entertaining an opinion, that they could amend their condition by violence, and by means of secret organizations. This necessarily put them in the power of designing and frequently profligate men, whose nods, winks, inuendoes and ambiguities became significant and full of meaning, which propagated deception from the necessity for confidence, and the danger attending discovery. This error cannot be too much deprecated; for, notwithstanding all the noise made by the Holy Alliance (and their abettors in this country) about the extent and danger of secret associations, beyond the age of clanship or religious enthusiasm, it is impossible that any secret organization can become sufficiently extensive, among the bulk of the people, to endanger a government of ordinary vigilance, or for any object of national utility against a bad one. The chances of discovery multiply with extension, and the diffusion of knowledge among the people is another bar to success; for, as it is not always accompanied with fidelity and integrity, the parties are more likely to calculate the danger, and also the advantage to be derived from betraying their associates*. Assuming, therefore, the principles to be correct, upon which secret political confederacies have been formed in this country, (which cannot be admitted for a moment,) it is astonishing that the repeated lessons the people have received, since the commencement of the French revolution, has not deterred them from such dangerous and preposterous attempts, from the palpable impossibility of eluding detection.

The disruption that has taken place in society, by the misapplication of the means of enjoyment, to an extent never equalled, in any nation, has divested the labouring classes of all power; leaving them insulated, defenceless, and alone; and, in such attempts, they have not only the whole strength and vigilance of government to combat, but also that of all the capitalists, employers, and idlers in the country. The remedy for existing evils must, therefore, be found in calm and deliberate discussion, to which the utmost possible extent of publicity should be given, and not in secret cabal. Experience has shown, that an immense mass of misery may co-exist with a government theoretically free, and from, apparently, the most opposite causes, England and Ireland, at the present moment, exhibiting the two extremes, of indolence and want of motive for exertion, and excessive labour, producing similar results. Ma-

* While endeavouring to dissipate the confederacy at Glasgow, including every expence, it only cost me twenty-seven pounds from the middle of December 1816 to the 22d of February 1817, when the men were so unnecessarily taken into custody, and had mere detection and punishment been my object, and not prevention, I could have induced any number that might have been required to disclose their proceedings at the expence of a pound a head.

chiavel's maxim, (which has been thought illiberal,) that men, when well governed, care little for liberty, may, without any great violation of truth, be extended a little farther, and conjoined with Pope's, that, when the mass of them live in comfort, they are as indifferent about *forms* of government.

It is questionable if the darkest settled despotism in Europe can exhibit a population who, with one-half the exertion, cannot enjoy more positive comfort than the labourers of Great Britain, the essence of whose boasted liberty consists more in the privilege of complaint than in action or fruition. Where the right of private property is at all respected, the comparative comfort and happiness of the bulk of a people are not incompatible with a pure and perfect despotism, the honours of the dungeon, the bow-string and the scimitar being generally reserved for the benefit of their superiors. This is, however, no argument in favour of despotism, nor a reason why checks should not be imposed to prevent the abuse of power, but it demonstrates that, frequently, more depends upon administration than on form, and that the evils in which we are involved are not necessarily interwoven with the frame of our government.

Those evils have arisen from various causes, and not a few of them from the errors of mere speculative, although benevolently disposed, men, the chief of which are as follows. Virtually assuming, that increasing the quantity of products by scientific invention can only throw a certain portion clear of labour, but cannot be so applied as to diffuse the benefits of cheaper production among the great body of the people. Exposing labour to the wildest system of combined and individual speculation, without reference to the comfort of the labourer, which, by pressing him down to the lowest possible means of subsistence, morally and physically degrades him, while legal and conventional restrictions confer special privileges which operate in favour of particular classes. Restrictions and duties upon importation enhance the value of subsistence, by forcing inferior soils into cultivation, which depreciates the relative value of our manufactured products and benefits other countries, at the expense of the British labourer, there being no reciprocity of equivalents. Mortgaging the revenue has, in a great measure, removed all restraint upon the profligate expenditure of government, and its immoral tendencies are infinitely more ruinous than the physical privations it has caused. It has reduced unprincipled gambling speculation to a system that has ramified itself into every department of business, and corrupted the nation to the very core, making money the only god of our idolatry. It has annihilated all public principle; for what would have been a national disgrace in the reign of Elizabeth, English capitalists have unblushingly supported,— the principles of despotism as liberally as those of liberty; like Shylock, the only condition being the necessary securities for the bond. It has diffused a self-interested frigidity that has benumbed and blunted the finer feelings, like a deadly mildew, its paralyzing influence having reduced the moral sympathies and social affections to a money value.

In justification of the oppression inherent in, and resulting from, this system, the evil has been ascribed to a fixed and immutable law of nature, that population has a tendency to increase in a ratio proportioned to the facility with which they can procure subsistence; the constant action and reaction of which principle must always regulate the price of labour, as privation diminishes and comfort increases the number of labourers. The people have, therefore, been triumphantly told, that they have the remedy in their own hands, by diminishing their numbers, which is a downright insult to men of understanding, when applied to a class who are once degraded. Granting, when every facility is given to the generative power, that men, in common with other animals, have a tendency to increase, it is not material whether on a geometrical opposed to an arithmetical ratio, or any other, but that at some point, in a given series, they will come to press against the means of subsistence. It only proves that, to insure the same degree of comfort, a check must then be put to the further augmentation of numbers; but it does not prove that it either is, or ought to be, effected by privation, vice and misery, when applied to beings possessing the power of ratiocination. Fact and experience exemplify the very reverse of the position; for, down to a very low point indeed, in the scale of existence, we find them operate in an inverse ratio, and as the most powerful stimulant to improvident breeding. The question, therefore, resolves itself into this; whether man should be placed under the government of his moral and intellectual faculties, or left the slave of his mere animal appetites and physical propensities.

The assumption that a high remunerating price for labour will, in the progress of a well-regulated society, continue to operate as a stimulus to population, is as false in theory as it is opposed to fact and experience. Fluctuating wages may produce that effect, but high stationary wages would have no such tendency. Quick transition, insecurity and uncertainty will, in the one case, lead to profligate indulgence, and in the other, by means of superior education, to foresight, frugality and temperance. The same result follows, when a population is pressed down to that point, where they have but a very small portion of present enjoyment, and no means of providing against future want. Admitting they had the means of elementary education, which they cannot, beings, subjected to incessant toil to procure as much food as will support life and enable them to continue their race, can have neither desire for intellectual enjoyment nor future calculation. Their gratifications must, therefore, be all physical. Stimulants, when they can be procured, are resorted to, to recruit the exhausted frame, and improvident breeding follows, as the necessary consequence of a blind indulgence of the strongest propensity of animal nature, which, at the lowest point, continues to operate with undiminished force. Excessive labour, scanty, unwholesome food and unhealthy occupation, will shorten the duration of life, and produce a quicker succession of beings, but it will not lessen the absolute number; on the contrary, the increase will continue, until they are reduced to prey upon the lowest garbage. Thus, the physical and mental process of degeneracy is confirmed and perpetuated, until brutality and ignorance render amendment or escape almost hopeless.

The condition of Ireland fully exemplifies the truth of this position, and causes, leading to a similar result, are in rapid progression in our manufacturing districts. During the last session of parliament, indeed, an English minister* triumphantly quoted the vast increase of production, in our greatest staple branch of manufacture, as a proof of national prosperity; but, were he as capable of appreciating details as, he asserted, practical

* Mr. Huskisson, in his speech on the silk trade, on the 8th of March.

men were incapable of generalization, he would find our cottons purchased at no less a price than the degradation of two millions of productive labourers. Let those, therefore, who consider such a system useful and necessary, to call forth the energies and develop the inventive faculties of man, pause and ruminate on the consequences. It is not very consoling to the benevolent mind, nor will it be popular with those who are dazzled with the splendor of the aggregate amount of our national resources; but it is not the less true that, by the direction they have received, the retrocession of the comforts of the great body of productive labourers has been on a ratio nearly corresponding to the amount of their increase. In proof and illustration, it was my original design to take a view of the *present* condition of our manufacturing and agricultural population, from documentary and other evidence, lately laid before parliament, chiefly with the view of benefiting the sufferers, by the majority of whom the combined operation of the evils, with which they are surrounded, seems to be very imperfectly understood; also to point out some of the advantages to be derived from a proper application of the repeal of the Combination Laws; but, having already exceeded my intended limits, I must reserve it for a separate and future opportunity. I shall, therefore, conclude with the well-known prophetic lines of the amiable Goldsmith, who, had he lived to the present period, would have seen them realized to an extent he could not contemplate.

> " Ye friends to truth, ye statesmen who survey
> The rich man's joys increase, the poor's decay;
> 'Tis yours to judge how wide the limits stand,
> Between a splendid and a happy land."

THE END.